To dear m...
love Jan
1.3.2001

MOTHERS
BEHAVING BADLY

MAGGIE GROFF

RANDOM HOUSE

Published by
Random House Australia Pty Ltd
20 Alfred Street, Milsons Point, NSW 2061
http://www.randomhouse.com.au

Sydney New York Toronto
London Auckland Johannesburg
and agencies throughout the world

First published 1999

National Library of Australia
Cataloguing-in-Publication Data
Groff, Margaret
    Mothers behaving badly.

    ISBN 0 091 84008 2.
    1. Motherhood–Humor 2. Motherhood. I. Title

306.87430207

Illustrations by Maggie Groff
Typeset by Midland Typesetters
Printed by Griffin Press Pty Ltd
10 9 8 7 6 5 4 3 2

In loving memory of my mother
MARION JOHNSON
A hard act to follow

ACKNOWLEDGEMENTS

Thanks to:

My husband and best friend Jay, a wonderful man who for twenty-two years has nurtured my dream to write.

My daughter Hannah Kay, the nicest person I have ever met, and without whom this book could not have been written.

My incredible father, Captain Herbert Johnson, from whom I inherited a dogged determination and a profound sense of the ridiculous. Thanks Pop for such a warm and happy childhood.

Stella and Jay Groff, my parents-in-law, for their fine example and love.

Noela Pretty, friend and typist, who deciphered my illegible scrawl, provided marvellous feedback and was my sounding board every step of the way.

Selwa Anthony, my literary agent, for help and encouragement above and beyond her percentage.

Alan Jones, radio broadcaster, who blazed the trail with his support and kindness.

Jody Lee, editor, who provided valuable assistance and has not mentioned the word 'deadline' once.

My dear friends Bambi Hanson, Rosa Piper, Ewa Felisiak, Alison

Morgan, Bette Cunningham, Lynn Gould, Dee Turner, Bernadette Countryman, Ruth Thompson, Fiona Porter, Anne Meates, Rosemary Rogge and Sylvia Brown who have provided invaluable advice, anecdotes, encouragement and friendship over more years than I care to remember.

Last, but not least, a big bouquet of carrots to my rabbit, Flopsy Bunny, for being my constant companion in this rather solitary business of writing. I have forgiven him for that little mishap on the first draft.

CONTENTS

Introduction
Addendum to Marriage Certificate

INTRODUCTION

I wrote this book for Miranda. One minute Ms Miranda was a Gucci-shod executive, chairing meetings and firing the non-compliant, and the next, WHOOSH, Miranda's brain came out with the placenta.

I watched idly from my neighbourhood perspective at the kitchen sink as Miranda tirelessly strove to maintain the trappings of corporate womanhood and the genteel life she had known. I gazed in horror as she washed 46 bath towels, 14 tablecloths and 70 nappies a week, and staggered round the garden walking into hanging baskets and tree trunks.

I listened to tales of sleepless nights, cafe lunches where George screamed, daycare centres where George caught colds, Miranda's need for intellectual stimulation, George being sick in the car, Miranda being sick in the car, building funds for private schools, house renovations, portacots, a mother's need to have time away from her children and let's not forget the biggy—quality time. Miranda's catastrophic maternal responsibilities knew no bounds. If Miranda could have faxed young George off to her own mother, she would have.

Miranda joined a book club, went to gym, had three massages a week and saw every foreign film at the Valhalla. She cut her hair and dyed it blonde, bought a cappuccino machine and a mobile phone and spent hours trying to book the highly gifted eight-month-old George into pre-school. Poor Miranda. The wheel was going round, but the hamster was dead.

The doggerel continued. Miranda missed George's first steps, his first words, the pre-school wouldn't take him, the babysitter hadn't read the right stories, the child psychologist said George was overeating because of maternal deprivation, the cleaner wasn't doing the bathrooms right, Santa wasn't true and it was wrong to lie to a child, George couldn't play the piano and was allergic to milk, cats, dogs and Miranda. On and on it went.

I wanted to shake her. Bash her senseless. Tie her to the washing line with her 46 towels and her 14 bloody tablecloths. How dare she! She, who had a wonderful loving husband, a beautiful home and a healthy child. She, who had been given the fruits of life to enjoy and nurture and had cast them aside for some pathetic misdirected ideal that intelligent, educated, important women were wasted on mother-hood.

It didn't help that she was pretty.

'Typical,' said my husband. 'You women are always complaining about other women. Why don't you go and help the poor girl instead of standing there bitching?'

So I did.

Miranda.

This book is for you.

GORGEOUS GEORGE

ADDENDUM TO MARRIAGE CERTIFICATE

I, _____ , knowingly understand I shall be tired for the next 20 years.

I accept the fact I will not have two logical thought processes in a row until I am 45.

Sign here _____

CHAPTER ONE

THE WONDER OF YOU

Motherhood is the hardest thing you will ever do. It has no parallel. But nature is kind. It has given us strength, intuition and capability. We just don't realise it. You see, mothers know a lot. Right from the start. It's the way the whole thing is set up in order for the human race to survive.

Even the venerable Dr Spock told mothers they know more than they think they do. I've got news for Dr Spock. I know a helluva lot more than he thinks I do, and I know a helluva lot more than I think I do. So do you.

What do I know? Well, for a start, I know exactly what those naughty bunnies on the right-hand side of the Bunnikins logo on the back of my daughter's bowl are doing. Yes. Knowledge is a powerful thing. Almost as powerful as motherhood.

DELUSIONS OF GRANDEUR

Pre-motherhood we fantasise our lives shall remain unchanged. We will be efficient female machines, incorporating the new little bundle into everyday doings. We'll show the rest how it's done. Perhaps we might teach the children at home. And work full-time, naturally.

For we are educated. The next generation of mothers. We will never wear tracksuits nor furry old slippers, and no child, especially our own, is going to dictate the conditions of our existence. What a riot!

THE TRUTH
(This bit is serious, so pay attention)

It is an extraordinary thing when someone you've never met before comes out of your body. It changes you completely. The perfect chrysalis, the confident organised career woman with a balanced life, transforms overnight, usually at 3 a.m., into a butterfly.

The butterfly is beautiful to everyone else, especially the tiny grub. But, to herself, the butterfly is shocked beyond belief and totally bewildered that her life is no longer her own. She is unprepared for the overwhelming power of her instinct to mother, as fierce and drawing as gravity itself, and she flaps her wings in chaos for many years, trying to be all things to all people, except herself.

This is motherhood. And the wonders and rewards are like nothing else on the face of this earth.

THE MYTH
There is no such person as Supermum, but Worrier Woman is alive and well. She's living at my house—and yours. Inside the safety of her four walls she rants and raves and frequently behaves in a manner more petulant and childish than her charges. Then off she goes, out the door, head in the air with a confident purposeful stride, a woman totally in control and coping marvellously with life. A woman to be envied by others who are inside their four walls ranting and raving and frequently behaving in a manner more petulant and childish than their charges.

THE MOTHERHOOD CLUB
Congratulations to us. We are members of the most exclusive club in the world, although few were impressed with the initiation ceremony.

I distinctly remember after the birth of my daughter telling 92 people the birth was fantastic, brilliant, the greatest experience I'd ever had. I lied. It was frightful. With a capital F.

In London, during the 70s, I was working at Kings College Hospital when Mary Quant, the fashion designer, gave birth. Within 15 minutes word spread through the hospital that Mary had said, 'It's like passing a melon!' Actually the jungle drums reported she had said 'shitting', but I don't want to be uncouth. Not yet, anyway.

I told myself, I must remember that. I didn't. I forgot. Sorry Mary Quant. I shall pay attention next time. You were the only one who spoke the truth.

I behaved like a barbarian during labour, horrified that despite months of antenatal instruction, I could not control my responses. I said dreadful things to my husband and worse to the luckless bozo

sitting between my legs. Poor nurse Bozo. Verbal abuse and a view of my fundaments, and all before breakfast.

I wore as a badge of capability, the fact I had only stayed in hospital for two days. The real reason I left early was that I was embarrassed by my behaviour—there were practically skidmarks on the lino on the way out. And the only badges I really wore were ghastly white vomit stains on the shoulders of every item in my wardrobe.

Why don't we tell the truth? Let's start saying, 'Good grief. That was terrible. I certainly deserve two weeks at Club Med Tahiti and that new Fisher and Paykel dishwasher with the two drawers at hip height, one each side of the sink . . .'

THE REALITY

It was day three when I lost the car in the car park at the shopping centre. Previously I had lost only keys, and always in exotic places like the Regent or the airport.

With every anxious step, my daughter screamed louder and my breasts tingled with milky pressure. It was horrendous. Eventually a rolypoly security man found my car—exactly where I had parked it.

Ten years on I still lose the car in the car park so I have devised a two-point plan:

Plan 1 I park the car sticking two feet out so that when I return I can look along a row and spot it. Often there is a man pointing furiously at my car. Unfortunately, now that I have told you, you will all be doing this and car parks the breadth of Australia will look like war zones.

Plan 2 I park in yellow 36 at Tweed City mall. This is my spot. If it is vacant I do the shopping. If not, I try later. Sometimes I'll risk 35 or 37, but it's not something I'd do willingly. I have written to the mall management suggesting they allocate places to local mothers, have signs saying Mrs Jones, Mrs Chin, Mrs Baker, like corporate office parks. I haven't had a reply yet.

I WANT TO PEE ALONE

I'm sorry to have to be the one to tell you, but Independence is just a town in Missouri, USA. You are now either the assisted or the assister. Often you're just the ass.

I was 41 when I went to the toilet alone. It was strange. I sat there feeling rather isolated, waiting for someone to fire questions at me broadside, tug at my jeans, or fall off the garden wall.

I think I was 43 when I remembered that normal people close the door.

GREAT LIES ARE TOLD IN SILENCE

Why didn't anyone tell me that having a baby was like a wildly passionate love affair, unrelenting in its continual power over the emotions. When your child first looks into your eyes the outpouring of love is so strong it's tangible, and the high is so up there it's in outer space. It is, quite frankly, so magnificent, it is indescribable.

And why didn't anyone tell me that a day would arrive when I would want to be hit by a truck, just so I could have a rest. Nothing too serious you understand, just enough to allow for four days in bed, with room service.

No one told me either that some days I'd want to drive the truck and ram it into half the population of Sydney.

So I'm telling you now.

THE CELEBRATION

We should rejoice in our wondrous abilities. Shout it from rooftops. When asked what you do, respond, 'I'm a mother' and add later that on Tuesdays you're a criminal lawyer. Put 'Mother' on business cards and passports and if people ask, 'Can you do this?' reply, 'Of course, I'm a mother.'

For, you see, there is nothing on this planet as exquisitely complex or as earth-shatteringly sensational as a mother.

Nothing.

CHAPTER TWO
THIS IS AN ADVERTISEMENT

WANTED   Mother!

REMUNERATION   Nil.

ESSENTIAL CRITERIA   Female.

DESIRABLE CRITERIA   Private income from family trust.

                                 Relative who owns a pub.

QUALIFICATIONS
Driver's Licence   Applicant must be able to control vehicle with broken air-conditioner in heavy traffic while listening to choking baby

in back seat. You will have the ability to concentrate whilst singing 'Incy Wincy Spider' and know the location of every public toilet on the eastern seaboard. You will have experience in loitering outside youth venues late at night.

Catering   You are capable of pre-planning menus for varied appetites for a minimum of 18 years. Supply of own milk to infants is required, as is frequent dinner preparation for 12 on an allocation of $40. You are able to make provisions for school fetes or charity drives, run a canteen for 400 and prepare packed lunches for people who won't eat them.

Paramour   You will be required to perform the dance of the Seven Target Towels after clearing evening refreshments. Toadying and fawning admiration of other senior management will be highly rewarded.

Administrator   Applicant will be directly responsible for control of budget estimates and utilisation of resources. You will field complaints and negotiate accordingly at great personal cost. Maintenance of communication network between management and non-management is required.

Nurse   Applicant must be able to go without sleep for six days whilst completing other duties and display proficiency in caring for the sick, particularly at two in the morning. Applicant should be on first-name terms with hospital casualty staff and be capable of holding down someone they love while someone else sticks a needle in them. Stain-removal ability is highly sought after in this category, as is knowledge of acne medication.

Sanitary Engineer   Applicant is responsible for collection and removal of refuse from kitchen to outside bin and weekly transportation of 52 kg bin up 50 steep stairs to point of council collection. Separation and haulage of recycling waste is required. This will be done at 5 a.m. because the person whose job it was forgot.

Early-Childhood Educator   Applicant must recite the complete works of A.A. Milne, know their times tables and be cognisant of everything that has ever been written anywhere about dinosaurs. The ability to make necklaces from macaroni and dental floss will be well regarded.

Teacher Applicant must be capable of working to deadlines. First year university mathematics is an advantage, as is knowledge of Japanese, the works of William Shakespeare, the complete structure of the Nile Delta and the construction of the Snowy Mountains Hydro Electric Scheme. Computer literacy is required.

Tailor Applicant will design and sew 22 rabbit outfits for the Christmas Concert. Other requirements will be repair and construction of school uniforms, fairy and ballet costumes, soft covers for musical instruments, bean bags and the embroidering of useless items as gifts.

Hairdresser Applicant will be required to detect and treat headlice, remove chewing gum from hair and cut a straight fringe whilst receiving verbal and physical abuse. Reparation is required of severe damage to hair design caused by scissor experimentation of the under-fives and occasional head shaving and/or restoration of socially acceptable colours for those who didn't read packet instructions.

Bike Engineer Applicant will need to be conversant with all aspects of bicycle maintenance, including fitting and removal of stabiliser wheels. Applicant must be able to recognise their offspring at a distance of two km, transform an ordinary bicycle into an armoured tank, repair punctures at a camping site 48 km from the nearest garage and convert Grandma's old wheelchair into a go-cart. A first-aid certificate is required.

Veterinary Assistant Applicant must care for and train a variety of pets after the owner has relinquished their position. Frequent feeding and cage cleaning is required and an ability to clip rabbit nails will be well regarded. Applicant must allow time for animals' exercise and be well versed in neighbourhood dispute resolution. Occasional burial services will be conducted.

Painter and Decorator Applicant will estimate paint quantities, purchase same and complete paintwork as other grown-ups in the house are allergic to the products. You will have the talent to transform four white walls into a Disney paradise or a smuggler's den and be conversant with removal of all sticky products and graffiti from behind bedroom doors. An ability to paint ceilings while cooking spaghetti bolognaise for six is an advantage.

Counsellor Applicant will be a good listener. You have the skill to successfully mediate between outside forces and family members, and the aptitude to negotiate between two four-year-olds who are fighting to the death over a marble. You will have the natural capacity to listen to in-depth superannuation discussions at 11.30 p.m., and successfully conduct friendships with a dear friend knowing your husband can't stand her husband. Counselling sessions will often be held while you are in the bathroom.

Telephonist Applicant will be able to field calls throughout a 24-hour period, give and take messages, and hold serious discussions on the telephone while someone is hanging off her left leg and yet another someone is chasing the cat round the kitchen whilst banging a tin with a wooden spoon. Applicant must provide sustenance to teenagers on the phone to avoid medical effects of prolonged stasis. The expectation is that you will receive several calls, whilst preparing dinner, from charities and tele-marketing agents selling you a four-day package holiday in Noosa.

Psychiatrist You will hold the equivalent of a first-class honours degree in psychiatry and be knowledgeable on 2400 methods of blackmail.

Landscape Gardener Applicant must be able to start a temperamental lawn mower, operate blunt gardening equipment and be capable of keeping house plants alive. You will know the phone number of the local poisons centre and be abreast of the latest methods in composting, pruning, seed cultivation and tree surgery. You will be able to arrange flowers with no stems in a vase and know the location of every mouse that has died and been buried in the last 20 years.

Entertainment Officer You will co-ordinate sporting functions by frequent use of the telephone and trips to the school office. You are required to coach games in all weathers and encouraged to enter into strong verbal discussions with opposing factions. Purchase and maintenance of extraordinarily expensive equipment is required. You will prepare successive annual parties, conduct exciting events whilst dressed as a fairy or Long John Silver, produce jellies covering the complete colour spectrum and invent games where everyone wins. And you will do Christmas.

THIS IS AN ADVERTISEMENT

A small person just came into the kitchen and told me if I don't let her go to Bridget's house, I will not be receiving a Mother's Day present. Blast!

CHAPTER THREE

HOW TO OVERCOME MATERNAL SELF-DOUBT THROUGH GRANDILOQUENCE AND DECEPTION

Okay, okay. So I let her go to Bridget's house.

Let's start on ways to build self-esteem. I hope you like the chapter title—I spent ages thinking it up. Practically the whole of speech night.

DISCARD EXCESS BAGGAGE

Like to lose three kilograms overnight? It's simple. Throw out your handbag. I'm serious. Go for a walk today and pick out mothers who look as if they know what they're doing. They have something in common. No handbag.

For years I carried a cavernous bag containing receipts, sweet wrappers, hair brushes, old envelopes with shopping lists on, keys to every house I'd ever lived in and a make-up bag equipped to paint the cast of *Aida*.

As time progressed I acquired the privilege of carrying other people's things—caps, gloves, toys, spare clothes, newspapers, glasses and oranges. So I bought a bigger bag. I was now carrying freight.

Then I met Maudie Reddy. Maudie was 75 and drove a beautiful old split-windscreen Mini Minor. One day she gave me a lift. I was surprised to see her casual attire of baggy jeans and holey jersey accompanied by a splendid Italian handbag. We climbed into the car and Maudie, with the proficiency of a pilot, prepared for take-off. She pulled out the choke on the dashboard, hung the handbag on the knob to stop it popping back in, and fired up the engine.

As we lurched and backfired up the road, Maudie shouted over the noise, 'Only use for a handbag, my dear, unless you're a fool or a fairy.' I haven't used one since.

Maudie also had a long stale French loaf on the passenger seat. When I enquired its use, she informed me the offside indicator had broken and if she needed to turn left, she stuck the French loaf out the window.

Now I wear clothes with pockets in which I carry a small purse containing driver's licence, credit card, small change, lipstick and bandaid. Sunglasses I push up on my head à la Jackie 'O'. I have never missed my handbag—not for a single second. Try it. It's wonderful. Like being a, you know, a father!

N.B. Do I hear bleating about bottles and nappies? Mothers! You are not focused. I'm talking about *handbags*. Obviously babies, picnics and beach trips require a large all-purpose bag.

SKULLDUGGERY JAM

I'm known in these parts for my jam. Occasionally people walk past me in the street and I hear them whisper, 'That's her, the jam lady.' Sometimes I even hear their dogs whispering, 'Did you see that fatso we just passed?'

HOW TO MAKE SKULLDUGGERY JAM

You will need:

Empty jars.
A large tin of brand name jam.
A tin opener.
Elastic bands.
Labels.
Calligraphy pen.
Pinking shears.
Red and white checked gingham.

Wash and dry empty jars. Open the tin of jam. Spoon jam into empty jars—you will have to chop at it a bit as tinned jam tends to be chunky and hard to settle. Screw on lids.

Now cut circles of gingham twice the size of the lid by using the pinking shears. Secure over lid with elastic band.

Finally use fancy writing to label your work. The date always adds a touch of authenticity. I have also been known to say I grew and picked the fruit myself.

DISCOVERY OF THE NINETIES

Two amazing things happened to me in 1990. Firstly I realised every time my husband said I looked awful, I was lying on the designer sheets I'd bought to match the decor. I held the sheets up to my face.

He was right. I looked as grey as a melted penguin.

Secondly I discovered that, although I failed abysmally to impress my husband, child, neighbours or anyone in the street, I had it in my power to completely mesmerise the sales assistant in the manchester department at Grace Brothers.

I did this by requesting a mirror, holding the bedding under my chin, and coquettishly moving my head from side to side. I knew what she was thinking, this Tracy with the Skinny Legs. She was thinking I was really somebody. A mother over 25 who actually, probably, no really, engaged in sex.

I never bought the sheets. Couldn't afford them. But, oh, the exhilarating feeling of having impressed a human being under the age of 20 was as beneficial to this tired old mum as a week at a health farm. **Motto:** Don't wear grey when over 30 and purchase bedding to make *you* look good, not the room.

QUESTIONTIME IN THE HOUSE

Working on the assumption your brain is partially addled and you have lost the ability for logical thought, I have prepared four answers that will cover just about anything you are asked. They will give an air of intelligence and allow deflection of conflict with confidence. Pin them on the kitchen cupboard and learn them by heart.

1.   Thank you for letting me know.
2.   We'll see.
3.   Because I'm the mother.
4.   What do you think?

They may prompt further discussion, but are an infallible first line of defence.
Test   Pick one of the above to match each question.

1.   Can I have a Bubblejet Barbie?
2.   Next time we go on holiday can you pour Pepsi in the snow so I can drink it?

3. Mum, come quick, Robert's puked on the roses.
4. Why can't I go to Sally's? You're the meanest mother in the whole world and I hate your guts.
5. Amanda Brown's got a Bubblejet Barbie.
6. When you kiss, where do you put your nose?
7. Mrs Hollins, your daughter has been very disruptive in class.
8. Why is it always you that gets to stay up?

THE ONLY CHILD

Oh dear! No matter the reason, intentional or nature's whim, the mother of a single child will experience guilt. You shouldn't but you will. The perception of a one-child family is somehow accusatory, a veiled inference you couldn't do it again. Questions such as 'How many children do you have?' and 'Is that your *only* child?' never fail to raise ire.

Once, in response to 'It's such a pity your daughter doesn't have a sister,' I replied, 'No, it's not. I'm Chinese. It's the law there.' Then I went out and chiselled the 'N' off the back of the stupid woman's Range Rover.

Only children are first children. They are successful, confident and self-motivated, have wonderful parental attention, a room to themself, rarely get bored and I wish I'd been one.

HOW TO SAY NO

Such a small easy word, but constant use reduces its effectiveness. After a while you begin to feel like a maternal harridan and people start pointing at you in the street saying, 'There goes old killjoy from number 7.'

When you are tired and trying to think, the word 'no' seems to roll off the tongue to every childhood request. Most of the time you don't even register the question. We all do this and we shouldn't because 'no' is rarely influential.

Try substituting my responses in 'Questiontime in the House' and save 'no' for important times like, 'Mummy, can I put my hand on this pretty red stove top?'

I nearly got caught a cropper on Friday. The ballet teacher sidled up to me and asked, 'Can you sew?' Visions of a million pink tutus flashed before my eyes. I looked her straight in the face and lied 'No.' It was very close.

And what of Tupperware invitations? Or the lingerie parties? Even the dreaded Girls' Night Out. It's fine if these occasions delight you, but brood mares like me seem to be forever cornered at the school gates with invitations I don't know how to refuse.

Many a night I've spent bored stupid by the benefits of plastic marinating dishes. Well, not any more. The new me says, 'Oh, how sweet of you to ask, but I'm afraid I'll have to say no as it's really not my thing. The best of luck anyway.' And, do you know, I'm no longer asked.

BE PREPARED

How often, in the morning, have you fed and polished children before stepping into the shower? You know the rest. The phone rings, someone can't find their homework, another needs precisely $4.50 for sport, a tradesman arrives and the dog escapes. Before you know it, you're standing in the queue at the supermarket looking like the wreck of the *Hesperus*.

In the next queue is a glamorous mother of five. You know this because she has disposable nappies and 12 litres of milk in her trolley. She is wearing designer jeans, a recognisable hairstyle and earrings. Often she is reading *Vogue* and eating an apple. She will not have a handbag.

You, on the other hand, look like a person who needs a month at the Ponds Institute, have plucked a trashy weekly from the stand and your stomach is rumbling because you didn't eat breakfast. You can't wait to get to the car and devour the chocolate biscuits.

It doesn't have to be like this any more.

The Solution

When you awake, don't speak to anyone or you will be asked to do something. Go straight to the shower and close the door. Wash, dress and do your hair without stopping. If there's time, slap on lippy. It won't wear off as you don't have time to eat until everyone else has gone, or are back asleep. Short of head injury and flowing blood ignore all attempts at interruption.

You are now ready for anything. Start tomorrow and don't waver. It will take a while for the household to stop sabotaging your intentions.

The Exclusion

You will not be able to do this if you are breastfeeding. The baby must come first. Jump in the shower with full breasts and a crying baby and you'll have white fountains to rival those of the Tivoli Gardens. Clever, but messy.

Sustenance

The only recognisable part of the word 'breakfast' for mothers is the 'fast' bit. 'Fast' as in 'go without' or 'fast' as in 'the speed of light'. Every time I see advertisements that show fond mamas sitting at breakfast tables en famille, tucking into a bowl of cereal, I want to give the ad executive a serious facial. We know it's the most important meal of the day—the two hours of nausea after we miss it tells us this. The answer has to be in lateral thinking.

Let's forget the stereotype breakfast—cereal, toast, coffee. We need something that can move around and be left for ten minutes. And preferably disgustingly healthy enough that no one else will pinch it.

Suggestions

Fresh fruit Cut into bite-size chunks in a bowl. Apple, orange and banana go well together. Carry it around with you and eat a bit when you want. When you've finished, drink a glass of milk. (Don't use tinned fruit, it's too runny and you can't use your fingers.)

Banana smoothie Remember to do this alone, otherwise everyone will want one and you'll be left with the dregs. Put a glass of milk, one banana, one tablespoon of malt and one tablespoon of honey in the blender and whizz. This is particularly good if you're feeling queasy in the mornings.

A SPOT OF CHOCOLATE CHEAT

I thought we'd finish this section with chocolate, so here is another bit of underhanded catering from Maggie's kitchen. This one's for Christmas—that's the time at the end of December when you try to make everything yourself.

CHOCOLATE CHRISTMAS LOG

You will need:

one store-bought chocolate Swiss roll.
one tin Betty Crocker Chocolate Fudge Icing.
icing sugar.
small decorations—Christmas tree, robins, etc.

The aim is to make it 'homemade'. Cut a 1 cm slice off the end of the Swiss roll. Lay the slice flat and cut into quarters. Now position one of the quarters on top of the Swiss roll so it looks like a knobbly branch. Stick it on with a bit of fudge icing. Eat rest of slice.

Next cover the whole log in fudge icing. It's sticky and fiddly and finger lickin' good. Don't smooth it flat—grade it with a fork to make it look like a log.

Sprinkle icing sugar through a sieve over the log to resemble snow. Pop on the ornaments.

Store covered in the fridge. Yummo!

CHAPTER FOUR

ORDER IN THE HOUSE

Caution: This is a big section—it's a big part of our lives.

You are forgiven for thinking maternal curves are prerequisite qualifications for tidying up, but without them human beings seem incapable of the task. Centuries of indoctrination have put this creative suffering in mother's court, and it is up to modern mum to do something about it.

We are not going to fight. Neither threat nor stealth will achieve co-operation, so why waste energy trying.

THE PERCEPTION
We must change the perception that a tidy home equates with our value as a mother. Unfortunately we perpetuate this each time we open a door and say, 'Come in, excuse the mess.' Often we qualify with, 'I've been busy doing tax returns.'

Modern mum knows that tax returns are important and a tidy house is not. But prehistoric mum, the self-conscious, is yelling full throttle, 'I should have tidied first.'

CUT AND PASTE TIME

Make three large signs saying: 'Don't apologise for the mess'

Put one on the front door, one on the back door and one by the phone as insurance for: 'Yes, come round now, but excuse the mess, I've just got in.'

DON'T APOLOGISE FOR THE MESS

Have you done it?

Good.

You have just taken the first step in changing things for your great-granddaughter.

Next we must look at our own perception of tidiness. Let's check some facts.

- People don't notice their own mess. Look around now. The mess is other people's, isn't it? The coffee cup, shoes on the floor and discarded paperwork are yours, but they are not, in your mind, part of the overall catastrophe. Odd, eh?
- Many mothers find it impossible to do other things until the house is tidy, courtesy of the aforementioned indoctrination. Whilst we know this thinking is wrong, it is nonetheless there, and we will deal with this in a moment.
- A tidy house is easier to keep clean. Unfortunately this is true.

So there you have it. A conundrum.

SENSIBLE ACTION
1. A Place for Everything

Go round the house and establish a place for everything. Remember, whilst something might be in its correct place, it doesn't have to be tidy in its place. This allows for a modicum of throwing things which can be most satisfying.

Examples:

- **Corkboard** Put a corkboard on the kitchen wall. Pin up all household paperwork—bills, begging letters from school, ads, vouchers—you know the sort of thing. The more higgledy-piggledy it is, the busier you look.
- **Videos** Place all videos in a big deep basket by the TV.
- **Shoes/boots** Place in a large plastic-lined basket by the back door.
- **Hats/caps** Establish a shelf area in the linen cupboard. Throw them all in and close the door.
- **Bits & pieces** Safety pins, old keys, coins, badges and whatnot go in a pretty bowl on the fridge where people under three feet can't see.
- **Toys** You open children's doors, throw hard and close quick. If this bothers you, imagine the room is one big basket.
- **Sporting equipment** I use the cupboard under the stairs. It's a danger zone. Smells, too.
- **Clothes** Over the banister—saves dusting. If you don't have a banister put up some hooks near the back door and hang it all up, pile upon pile.
- **Dirty clothes** (I have two laundry chutes . . . oh smug me.) Don't have laundry baskets in bathrooms. This involves bending down twice—once to pick up off the floor, once to get it out of the basket. You just have to go round each morning and gather up. Then you hurl it through the laundry door and shout, 'Take that you filthy bastards.'
- **Ironing** This should be kept in a locked cupboard at the back of the shed, because it's always there, in your face, if you leave it anywhere in the house. Put it all on the bottom shelf of the linen cupboard. This way you have to get down on your hands and knees to see it.
- **School bags** These little darlings gravitate to the side of the fridge in our house. They are A1 for tripoverability. You

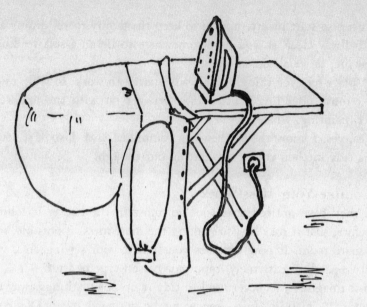

SOMETIMES WHEN I'M IRONING SHIRTS I
THINK 46 IS A GOOD AGE FOR A WIDOW.

point your pointing finger and say, 'Go to your room.' Then
you pick it up and hurl it through the owner's door.

- **Photographs** of friends' children that you haven't seen for
  20 years. Straight in the old shoebox for photos of friends'
  children that you haven't seen for 20 years.
- **Books/newspapers** These should be everywhere. Preferably in front of faces. You shouldn't be putting these away at
  all.
- **Recyclables** And don't we know about these. I've tried the
  environmental bit, three bins in the kitchen, and whilst
  saving the world I destroyed my own environment. Now it
  all goes into one kitchen bin and I divvy up outside if it's
  not too gungy.

2. Aim to Keep Communal Areas Clear
We have to solve the little 'indoctrination' problem of needing to tidy
the house before getting on with other things. This could take

centuries so start by attempting to keep the family room, dining area and hallway clear, so you have somewhere to lie on a sofa reading a magazine, as we all do so often.

'A place for everything' has already started to work, so whip round and remove offending articles and then get on with the important letter, painting, whatever.

Yes, yes, I know the kitchen is a communal area. Listen, if you've got a tidy kitchen you're not getting out enough.

3. Confine Your Mess/Work

You may have noticed that you 'do' most in the house. It follows, therefore, that it may be you making the most mess. If possible, seize the spare room. It now becomes your office, your sewing area, your creative patch of extremely important person type of stuff.

Just imagine, you never need to tidy it up or put things away and because the mess is yours, you won't be bothered by it. Don't you dare put the ironing in there.

If you don't have a spare room, set up a large table in the family room and put a sign saying 'Mine' above it. Don't even think of tidying that table up. It's a workplace not a showplace.

N.B. Think seriously about abandoning the 'formal lounge' nonsense—it's nothing but a subversive method by male architects to perpetuate the myth that a home requires a spectacularly tidy room in which to entertain guests. It doesn't give you a place to go and relax away from the children because:

- You don't want to be away from the children, you want them to be away from you.
- The things you need to relax with are never in that room.
- All guests congregate in the kitchen anyway.

Commonsense should tell you that if you have two living areas, they should both be family rooms.

4. Always Put Things Back Where You Expect To Find Them

This works. The hard part is getting others to do it. Often, my six-acre voice can be heard calling, 'Where is the stickytape? I want it now.' Thunderous hooves steam down the hall and, miracle of miracles, the stickytape is back in the stickytape drawer. By the time kids leave home they should be putting things back nicely.

5. Never Go Anywhere Emptyhanded

Invaluable. Teach the children and you will have passed on a remarkable living tool. It is effective in all aspects of life and work. Start small. You are in the kitchen. The post arrives. As you go to the mailbox, take the kitchen garbage with you and dump it in the outside bin. You have now completed two chores in a little over the time it would take to complete one.

Effective time management such as this will help what's left of your brain work for your tired old legs.

Trouble Shooting

- **Teenagers'** rooms are a health hazard. Do not tidy. You may find something you don't want to know about (unless you suspect drugs, in which case, rip it apart). Keep door closed to contain the smell. A good clean twice a year with industrial-grade chemicals should suffice, and let the dog in on a regular basis to scavenge pizza from under the bed.

- **Men** Most family members are highly creative in mess design and location, and adult males seem genetically predispositioned to create small repetitive messes, such as: wet towels on beds, beard shavings on soap, newspaper print on walls, axle grease in sinks and empty leftover plates in the fridge. This will drive you up the wall.

    Twenty years of veiled threats will not force one man to pick up one pair of underpants off one floor. Much better to pick them up yourself, and then clean the bath with their face washer. We shall not discuss what men do to the kitchen when cooking their 'specialty'.

- **Children's rooms** Whoa! Only thing to do here is regard the room as a whole house and confine mess to its own 'like' pile. I use K-Mart plastic boxes—one for dolls, one for horses, etc. Children's rooms need a good clear-out once a year, but keep detritus for two weeks in case of: 'Mum, have you seen a little pink dinosaur made of paper?' Unless your child is asthmatic, children's rooms only need dusting and vacuuming every two to three weeks and each time you do it you'll be surprised at how dirty they are. Tip: 'Mummy's going to vacuum your room tomorrow, so would you clean up the tiny bits off your floor', will see a frenzy of activity. Important bits of paper, Lego parts, leaves, slides, doll earrings, tank parts and half-inch crayons will be swept to higher parts for fear they will disappear into the vacuum, up the electrical lead and into that great void beyond where all missing things live.

- **Littlies**   Young children like to play where you are. By day's end the house is a toy shop. Tell them to take everything to their room, and then do it yourself while they wander off. This is not how you would like it to be—but it is how it is. Don't lose sight of the desired end result—toys away, calm mother, happy child. Never say you will throw away their toys if they don't tidy up. This is wicked. Mummies are never wicked . . .

- **Tidy Mary**   The stock is dissolving in a jug. You are frying onions. It's precision casserole cookery. Tidy Mary is the helpful person who tips the stock down the sink and washes up the jug. Tidy Mary also throws away shopping lists.

- **The major obstacle**   The man of the house! Strange, isn't it? He, who has never tidied up, has no intention of tidying up and wouldn't know how to do it in a Hobbit's age, starts barking around the house about children tidying their rooms. Many a weekend of exalted promise has been ruined in this fashion and I, for one, have no idea what to do about it. Phrases such as 'straight to the Tower of London' and 'off with his head' spring to mind.

- **Inefficiency**   There is a tendency by those who have waved the last sprogling off to school, to stretch the housework/tidy lark to fill the whole day. You will be excused for two months. This is the time it takes to absorb the deliciousness of having 25 hours each week when you can complete a sentence, a phone call or a task without interruption. After that you need to pep up the time-management skills.

HOW TO TIDY UP THE MAGGIE WAY—QUICKLY

- Pick one table top in a central spot to act as your repository for everything. Get in the habit of putting all stray items on it—basketballs, library books, homework, half-finished drawings and things to be fixed. This confines small messes to one large mess which you will learn to overlook. I use a trolley in my kitchen.
- Play a game. Go round the house and put away ten things in every room. Strays in the wrong room go on the repository table. Sometimes I vary this to be 100 things in the whole house, but I cheat and count the cutlery from the dishwasher.
- Another game with other players. This only works with under tens. Everyone else makes rude gestures at you behind walls. Tell the players to stand by the repository table. Then you shout, 'David, put the home readers in your school bag and report back to me. Charlotte, put the cap in the linen cupboard and report back to me.' Think one chore ahead to avoid staff wandering off.

When to Be Bossy

- When you are tired and emotional, the dog has vomited on the carpet and the house is awash with toys, clothes and smelly sneakers, known as hummers. No one, except the dog, will take the slightest bit of notice of you. You will feel guilty about upsetting the dog.
- When family members (except you) have allowed their mess to stray from their allocated mess areas, i.e. their rooms. Announce that *unlike other mothers* you don't mind their rooms being untidy, but they must remove their project from the dining room table this instant.

N.B. Tired children will react badly to this. Remember the desired result, and say '*Unlike other mothers* I don't mind if your room is a mess, but don't leave that project on the dining room table.' Then you put them in a warm bath and clear the table yourself.

CHAPTER FIVE
HOUSEWORK

HOUSEWORK CIRCA 1915

'It is considered perfectly acceptable in these times, once the house is clean and tidy, and the washing and ironing put away, for the housewife to take a short nap and lie on the kitchen floor.'

I found this in the housework section of an old American book of the 'Enquire Within Upon Everything' genre. I expect the woman who wrote it is dead. I certainly hope so.

HOUSEWORK CIRCA 2000

Q. Do you know why it's called 'housework'?
A. Because 'fuck' had already been taken.

Let's get something straight. Housework has nothing to do with motherhood. Housework is caring for a house. If you lived on your own you'd do housework. Those who reside in mud huts do housework. Anyone can do it. It's menial. If you can afford it, you should pay someone else to do it. Just like the Queen.

The washing and cooking are not housework. If you think they are, you are not able to separate housework and motherhood. Consider the following lists.

Housework	Motherhood
Caring for the House	Caring for the Family
Dusting	Washing clothes
Cleaning toilets	Shopping for food
Cleaning bathrooms	Shopping for children's clothes
Polishing	Cooking
Vacuuming	Sewing concert costumes
Washing windows	Getting up at 2.30 a.m. to tend
Defrosting fridge	the sick
Wiping mirrors and pictures	Ironing
Wiping out oven	Making school uniforms
Cleaning kitchen	Taxi service
Sweeping	Helping with homework
	Washing sheets/changing bed linen
	Etcetera, etcetera, etcetera

These things you do to or for the house. Family members benefit INDIRECTLY from these activities.

These things you do to or for the family. Family members benefit DIRECTLY from these activities.

Ten bucks says you never analysed this before. The difference is quite profound, isn't it? They are, obviously, two separate jobs. As I've said, anyone can do housework. Motherhood, on the other hand, requires skill, patience, and a variety of talents that are, quite simply, unlistable in their magnitude.

THAT DIRTY WORD

Let's blame the word 'housewife'. Blame. Blame. It has single-handedly created the misconception that both jobs, housework and motherhood, are one and the same, thereby laying the foundations of an insidious devaluation of motherhood as a profession.

Yes, it is a filthy word all right. I want you to go, right now, and remove it from your dictionary with a black marker.

Understanding the fundamental difference helps us focus on motherhood. It empowers us and provides ammunition to target the ravings of corporate woman who 'couldn't bear to stay home all day'. It allows those of us who work and juggle all three jobs to reassess priorities and concentrate efforts and hopefully alleviate the confusion of stress. It lets mothers with young babies feel comfortable spending time cuddling their child rather than vacuuming the carpet.

LATERAL THINKING

If both parents are employed, the job of 'housework' should be:

1.   Shared 50–50 (Yeah—right!);
2.   Done by a third party, i.e. a cleaner.

If one parent is employed the job of housework should be:

1.   Done by unemployed party (it is inconceivable that your family is so dirty it requires 40 hours of housework a week);
2.   Done by a third party, if you can afford it.

If neither of you is employed, the job of housework should be:

1.   Shared 50–50. This situation arises during periods of unemployment and on retirement. As far as I'm aware women still do it all in these cases. We must change this. (Another book right there.)
2.   Done by a third party if you can afford it, which you can't.

LITERAL THINKING

These are not the ravings of a feminazi. It's what's fair. Any other balance reduces your ability to perform motherhood properly.

We don't need university research to tell us women still do the lion's share of housework, whether they work or not. Bra burning, left-wing anti-male aggression and murder haven't worked. We must be moderate but firm. Working mums address the problem by hiring a cleaner. Non-working mums ensure they and their spouse understand clearly the difference between housework and motherhood and accordingly reduce the expectations on the polishing side of things to concentrate on nurturing their offspring. Children would rather come home to a warm homemade banana cake and a parent who can listen to their home reader than a chemically sterile toilet and sparkling dishes.

And ask yourself this: 'When I am very old, with trembly, spotty hands and varicose veins like sewer pipes, will I look back and wish I'd kept a cleaner house?'

Exactly!

I DO IT MY WAY

Some folk put aside a day for cleaning, but I couldn't bear to earmark a day of my life this way. Just imagine if you cleaned on Monday and on Tuesday someone walked sand through the kitchen. I'd be distraught!

I'm very much an 'as required' sort of cleaner, leaning heavily towards the 'get it next time' school of thought. And my house isn't dirty. It's just right. I mean, I wouldn't be embarrassed if a passing Jehovah's Witness needed to use my bathroom. I wouldn't let them, but I wouldn't be embarrassed if they did.

PLAY DESERT ISLAND DICKS

Try to do something with your brain while cleaning.

•   Listen to talkback radio—you'll get annoyed and clean faster.

- Think about what to get Amelia Rose Fotheringham for her birthday.
- Plan dinner for three nights.
- Play Desert Island Dicks—you have to imagine which eight men you'd want to sleep with if left on a desert island.

N.B. Small children in the house? Ha ha! You won't be able to do any of the above. You won't be able to clean, either . . .

HEALTH WARNING

Housework can be dangerous. Stroll down the cleaner aisle in a supermarket—there's a health warning on every product. Soon we will see 'HOUSEWORK CAN KILL YOU' on packets of soap powder.

Ever since I passed out demoulding the shower I have kept a curb on the cleaning cupboard. (I'd prefer a padlock with a lost key, but what can you do?) I'm not into vinegar and elbow grease either. I take the middle road. I will go to my ever-so-high-up-very-safe-out-of-reach cupboard and list the equipment.

- Dishwashing powder
- Washing-up liquid
- Blue sand bucket (stolen from Cammeray Golf Club) containing bleach and cloth for cleaning toilet
- Furniture polish
- Five rubber gloves with holey fingers (Year 3 science experiment)
- Cream cleanser
- Bleach
- One and a half dead cockroaches
- Two plugs
- Two old tea towels (dusters)
- Disinfectant

That's all folks!

I am 47 48 35 years old and have never owned:
- A toilet brush (filthy things)
- An ironing board (old towel and sheet on the table)

- Tupperware
- Blue water in the toilet
- A carpet sweeper
- A mop
- Plastic wrap
- A carpet shampoo vacuum thingy
- Air freshener toadstool doodad
- Those funny round tin pictures you put on hot plates
- A stove top I can see my face in
- A deodorised carpet

Think of the money I've saved. I should add, too, that I haven't washed a kitchen floor in four years. We live in the tropics and have a cork floor. It gets washed every time children run from the pool to the toilet. Usually I wipe up the spills with a guest's pool towel. I think polishing it could be dangerous, don't you?

FREE ADVICE

- Don't put anything in the middle of the most frequently used table—you will be forever moving it.
- Decorate the fridge. Why are fridges white? Mine is blue and white with little ducks all over it and you can't see the paw prints (instructions later).
- Clean the front door. First impressions and all that jazz.
- Put small ornaments in a box marked 'For Retirement'.
- Remove houseplants. They are dust traps and always in some stage of disease or death.
- Have windows cleaned professionally twice a year. Any real estate agent will tell you that if windows are clean the whole house looks sparkling.
- Like windows, clean basins give the impression of total makeover. Each morning I wipe them out with the last person's towel and then hang it up for them. I'm so thoughtful.
- Never vacuum alone. There is no point in zooming around the floor plan without annoying anyone but yourself. Let them

see what a ghastly job it is. Suck up their papers, sabotage their phone calls.

- Don't swap homes with a friend for holidays—the children will break something equivalent in dollar value to two weeks in the Cayman Isles. You will be in a constant state of alert and spend the last two days cleaning—and more thoroughly than you would at home, too.
- Never leave the ironing where you might see it.
- Never do today what you can put off until tomorrow.
- If you have a daughter, make a large sign that says 'MARRY MONEY' and place it over her bed. This will ensure she will be able to afford to pay someone else to clean for her.

TROUBLE SHOOTING

School Holidays

Tempted as I am to say 'stuff it' to housework during holidays, this doesn't work. Family, lots of friends and house guests equates with lots of dirt. Delegation of tasks won't work either. I get rid of everyone each four to five days and whizz round and do the basics in a frenzy before they get back.

The Basic Frenzy

- Take phone off the hook.
- Wipe down communal areas—hall, lounge, dining, kitchen and family room.
- Vacuum communal areas plus bathrooms.
- Clean sinks.
- Clean toilets.
- Put flowers in vase in kitchen where you can see them.

It takes about two hours. If you don't do this you will be depressed by an insurmountable workload when everyone's gone. By the way, don't clean guests' rooms—it's rude to invade their space and you might find the present they've bought you and spoil the surprise.

COMPLAINTS

If you live with Felix from *The Odd Couple* and comments are made about low-calibre cleanliness, hand dear Felix a dustpan and brush and say, 'Feel free'. Don't you dare spend 40–50 years of your life pandering to someone else's standards and expectations. Be Oscar, and be proud.

HOW TO HIRE A CLEANER

I don't mean how to place the ad. You know that. I'm talking about resistance from Blind Freddy. Men come up with a million reasons not to have domestic help—'My mother had four children and she worked on the farm and she didn't have a dishwasher'—that sort of thing.

Naturally you could point out his mother impaled his father with a pitchfork, but you won't, because domestic help, if you both work and can afford it, is not negotiable.

Women who work at home in the family business will have a bigger fight. Blind Freddy will sulk. For weeks. Don't enter into feminist arguments. Hire someone for four hours and tell Freddy it's only two. Ignore the sulking and be particularly pleasant for several weeks to show Freddy it's money well spent.

THANK YOU

A very big one to that small battalion of men who help with the housework, especially when you have a new baby. Cherish them. They are ahead of their time. Why am I thanking men for doing what they ought? It's simple. If you don't, they won't do it again.

Renovating The Fridge

You will need:

Five rolls 45 cm wide Contact.
Methylated spirits.
Scissors.
A table.

Two hours alone.
A pin.
Tea towel.
A red pen.

Take the phone off the hook. Wipe all grease off the sides and door with methylated spirits. Allow to dry.

Start on the side you can't see and work from the back forwards. Don't allow excess to smooth round corners because this will curl (as you won't have cleaned round the corners properly).

Cut the serrated top of the Contact roll straight. Now position it to touch exactly the top edge and mark the bottom edge with the red pen. Turn Contact right-side down on table and cut straight across.

Peel about 30 cm of the top down and position on fridge.

Smooth over with tea towel. Now pull backing down in 30 cm tugs and continue, smoothing until it's all on. If you've made a mess (first-timer) you can peel it off and try again. Bubbles can be popped with the pin and smoothed out.

Then you cut the next. And so on.

If you get 'corner peel' stick it down with superglue.

Rust spots on white bits still showing at the edges can be camouflaged with Whiteout correction pen.

CHAPTER SIX

THE LAUNDRY by M.J. Groff, Dr of Washing

When I was a student in London, we used to put our washing in the bath, drink a gin and tonic, and stomp up and down on the clothes singing 'Tapestry' by Carole King.

Now I have a laundry. It's such an Australian thing. The British keep their washing machine in the kitchen and the Americans hide theirs in the basement, but here, in Magic Land, we have a room. It's so decadent. And nice to know we are ahead in laundrotech.

THE LAUNDRY CHUTE

We have two. It's why we bought the house and the only thing I've ever had to boast about. Did I mention I have two? Yes, that's right, two.

One chute falls from the pantry, the other from the bathroom. The clothes go everywhere because the shelf isn't up yet (naturally). Even Flopsy Bunny descends for an eiderdown landing. The brainless bit of fluff shoots across the floor like Olive Oyl, tears up the stairs, and waits expectantly at the top for another go. He prefers the pool slide if given a choice.

If you live in a two-storey house, you should consider a laundry chute. They save loads of time and provide hours of entertainment for children. But, please, put a shelf underneath.

SOAKING

Don't soak clothes in the laundry tub. You'll need it for something else before the stains are out. Use a bowl or bucket—and put this in the sink out of reach. I use a tall flour bucket that I borrowed from a horse in Terrey Hills who had borrowed it from a baker in 1986. I keep a constant solution of Napisan in it, which seems to get most things out. I change it monthly, sort of.

THE WASHING MACHINE

As a general rule, the more complex the machine, the more there is that can go wrong. All you need are the basics—hot, cold and warm water, low, medium and high water level and a strong and gentle cycle with a good spin. The rest is codswallop. We are washing clothes with this machine, not using it for open heart surgery.

FRONT LOADERS

Who thought of this? You cannot open the door of a front loader once the cycle has started—obviously the water would go all over the floor. So what do I do with the dirty sock I just found on the stairs and the school uniform from yesterday's sleepover bag? And you have to bend down!

BUYING A NEW MACHINE

Don't listen to advertising or be swayed by sales. Phone two laundrettes and ask them what machines they have, which washes the best and which breaks down the least. Take your list to a white goods dealer and check the machines for size and suitability. Go home and phone two other dealers to check prices. Call the one with the best price on the machine you've chosen and tell them you want free delivery if you buy today. Sometimes you can negotiate lower with cash.

SOAP POWDERS

Modern powders are very strong. Residue left in clothes and bedding irritates skin and causes rashes on babies, children and adults, particularly at sweat points and in the knicker department.

Babies' clothes and bedding should be washed in pure soap, such as Lux flakes. Stains can be soaked in the Napisan horse bucket first. The easiest way to use pure soap flakes is to dissolve them in a jug of hot water, add this to water in the machine, run machine ten seconds to mix it in, and then add the clothes. Think before adding softener to babies' clothes—more chemicals.

A very wise old woman (Maudie Reddy, she of Mini Minor fame) told me that the amount of time a product was in contact with a cleanser was more important than the force used. How right she is.

I soak everything in the washing machine at least two hours before I turn it on. This allows me to use less powder. Serious stains get a day in the horse bucket first.

SOFTENERS
Personally, I couldn't give a flying fart if my family scratched their faces on the towels.

SHARING A MACHINE WITH THE BODY CORPORATE
I did this for seven years. It was hell. No mother likes their precious baby's things going in a communal machine, to be washed where old Ma Taylor in 4B has had her undies. The logistics of only doing a family wash on Monday and Friday are mindblowing.

My suggestion is to hire a simple machine that can go in the bathroom or be wheeled to the kitchen sink. Don't tell the neighbours because someone will complain. You will become very knowledgeable on plumbing attachments.

CREATIVE STAIN REMOVAL
Grease I use car engine degreaser, which you get in a can from K-Mart. Spray on grease, wait one minute, rinse well with cold water. It smells very bad so you have to soak item for a week but, hey, the stain comes out. I have used this on silk too, but please be very careful.

Grass Sponge with cloth soaked in methylated spirits.

Glue Soak in white vinegar for two hours, then wash in hot soapy water.

Rust Equal parts salt and cream of tartar (usually near the flour in the supermarket). Rub on wet rust stain. Leave in sun to dry and then wash normally. Repeat until stain has disappeared.

Ballpoint ink Sponge with methylated spirits, then wash.

Urine   Half cup of salt to 1200 ml of warm water or two tablespoons of white vinegar to 250 ml of warm water. Soak for two hours then wash normally.

Chewing gum   Put ice on gum and peel it off when solid. You can also put the clothing in the freezer for a few hours. (No wonder people think mothers are mad.)

Baby stains   Napisan will do it all.

Tips

- If you have had to use methylated spirits, don't wash de-stained item with anything else or it will all smell.
- When you have dyed the entire white wash pink with a red serviette from a pocket, don't panic. In the great scheme of things it doesn't matter—there are wars going on, you know. Add half a cup of bleach to a full load of water and re-wash the clothes immediately, running the wash cycle twice.
- Don't forget to remove worms, cicadas and sweets from pockets.
- Don't overwash. It isn't necessary to wash everything that turns up. (I have been known to shake talcum powder on the odd T-shirt and put it back in a drawer.) Is it necessary to use tablecloths? Ask yourself some serious questions . . .
- Tissues. A common occurrence. Shake off the fluff when dry and then blot with stickytape.

DRYING IT ALL

When I was a child, in the South Downs of England, drying the washing was a ceremonial performance. My father was a Master Mariner and had acquired two ship's masts which he established one each end of the garden to support the washing line. The line then had to be attached by a lanyard at either end, and raised on a pulley system, like hoisting a sail. You pegged out at half mast and then hoisted it all upwards. Our washing was a landmark for local aircraft flying, as it did, 40 feet above the house. Imagine how I felt when I saw my first dryer.

Options

Dryer   Invaluable if you have a baby, live in an apartment or a cold wet climate. Unfortunately they are expensive to run, shrink some items and reduce the life expectancy of clothes. You should never go out and leave the dryer on.

Outside line   Great for sheets and towels and jolly good exercise with all that bending and stretching. Not suitable for busy mothers in temperamental climates where there are mosquitoes and sandflies. It's also ill-gotten booty for passing thieves.

Inside line   Every mother should have one in the garage. A big one that pulls out from the wall. So what if the towels take three days to dry.

A dress rack in the laundry   Wonderful. Use wire hangers and hang everything up. This is a quick, efficient method of 'hanging out', reduces ironing and you don't have to worry about the weather. It has the added benefit of allowing certain clothes to go straight into the wardrobe, hanger and all.

A proper clothes rack   Good for undies and socks and anything else you can't put on hangers. Stand it next to the machine so you don't have to walk far.

Did I mention that I have two laundry chutes?

CHAPTER SEVEN

STORYTIME FOR MOTHERS—
'HAVE YOU SEEN MY ... ?'

Currently I can be brought to boiling point by a nauseating portrayal of breakfast in suburbia. Father is wiping dishes. Ha! The teenage sap are exchanging caustic comments. What is mother doing? Of course. She's fully dressed and lipsticked, and sitting down eating her breakfast. Yes. Sitting down! She is either smiling or someone from the props department has forced a coathanger in her mouth.

May I ask, do you smile between 7 and 9 a.m.?

In our house we set aside these two relaxing hours to play a particularly jolly game called 'Have You Seen My ... ?' This morning's round commenced when my husband bellowed,

'Have you seen my shoes?'

'They're in the kitchen where you took them off,' I called back. This was not good enough. He did not find them. I elaborated.

'They're in the kitchen. It's the room next to the lounge on the west side of the house and the shoes are on the floor next to the fridge which is the big blue and white mother where you keep beer. Your shoes are brown with laces.'

He then said, 'I can't see them.' This was because (a) the cat was lying on them; (b) someone had placed a schoolbag over them; or (c) he was still in the bedroom.

Next came, 'Have you seen my blue socks?' I did not remark on the fashion ethics of brown shoes/blue socks. He's American and not long out of crimplene trousers.

'They're in your sock drawer,' I yelled. 'The top right-hand drawer of the chest.' No matter he has kept his socks there for 20 years.

'They're not there,' he shouted, unable to move as a passing Viking had attacked him with a cutlass and rendered his legs inoperative.

I went to his side. We both stared in the drawer. The socks were not there. This is because they were in the laundry basket. Had I not been preparing three different breakfasts, school lunches, answering the phone, unloading the dishwasher and finishing homework, I would have had time to retrieve the socks, fold them in a professional manner and secrete them at the far corner of the drawer so I could exclaim, 'You just don't look, do you?'

A short wait elicited, 'Have you seen my keys?'

'No,' I answered cautiously.

There was a great thumping about and opening of cupboards. They weren't found. That's because they were in the car where I'd left them. There followed a short lecture on insurance and irresponsibility.

'Have you seen the butter?' he asked, waving dry toast in the air.

'It's in the washing machine,' I snapped.

'No, it's not,' he said. 'It's in the fridge.'

'Oh,' I replied. 'I thought you said "Have you seen the red beach towel Aunt Marjorie bought you for Christmas?"'

He looked at me with pity. I looked at him with pity. And marvelled at nature's foresight in making his arms just the correct length so he can check a squillion times a day that his most precious possession is right there in his pants where it was ten minutes ago.

CHAPTER EIGHT
EXERCISE

Exercise doth tiredness make whilst resting soothes the savaged soul.
WILLIAM SHAKESPEARE
(not really, I just made that up)

Exercise keeps you fit, and the fitter you are, the more you can do. Isn't it extraordinarily lucky that mothering is the most strenuous exercise routine ever devised? How else would we be fit enough to carry the heavy baskets to and from the car at family picnics?

The word 'exercise' indicates the concentration of specific movements within an allotted time whilst dressed in an outrageously expensive outfit appropriate to the task.

But wait a minute. Isn't shopping exercise? Haven't you walked three miles? Sure you have, but no one dares call it exercise because you weren't wearing cross trainers and prancing along as though a coconut was stuck in your bottom.

Be prepared. The next time someone asks, 'Do you exercise?', lower your eyes and say, 'Oh, yes, I'm a mother, I exercise a lot.' You may need to practise this in a mirror to achieve proper cause and effect.

THE NEW MOTHER ROUTINE

This is equivalent to six aerobic classes, and Robyn at the local gym couldn't hold a candle to you for sheer stamina. The only reason you don't look like Robyn is genetics and a whole lot of money. And, of course, you're wearing a stained nightie.

One hundred knee bends hanging out the nappies, a bit of pec strengthening with the vacuum and a quick power walk with the stroller are but a small proportion of the daily workout. Think of your body as one of those new chrome machines you can get for three easy payments. Think of the money you're saving. And just for fun, try folding yourself away in a cupboard . . .

POST-NATAL EXERCISES

It's important to do these and someone somewhere in this great country of ours will have told you how to do them. They are designed to return the inner workings to pre-assault conditions.

The most important exercise is where you tighten muscles in your pelvic floor (between the legs) and hold it for ten seconds before relaxing. You must do this often. If you don't you will wet yourself each time you laugh for the next 50 years.

I still do pelvic floor exercises at traffic lights, usually watching the man in the next car pick his nose. I expect I have the strongest pelvic floor muscles in the southern hemisphere.

UNPROFESSIONAL ADVICE FOR A NEW MOTHER

At some point a well-meaning, interfering, so-called professional, who has been eating stupid pills, will advise you to take regular exercise. Terms such as 'self-esteem', 'getting your body back into shape' and 'make time' will roll off certified tongues. You are excused for wanting to rearrange their hairdo with a bit of two by four.

There is no time to make and you are permanently tired because you never stop 'exercising'. I suggest you hang up the guilty hat on their ignorant nose and spend some quality time with a glass of shiraz.

I listened to advice. Silly me. I joined a gym—took out a six-month subscription. I spent 24 weeks asleep in the car outside and never went through the doors. It was wonderful.

TENNIS

How do you tell a St Ives mother at a funeral?
She's the one in the black tennis dress.

As well as exercise, tennis is companionship and entertainment. It does wonders for your temperament, too—I used to draw my husband's face on all three balls. I probably only made one in five games due to:

Chicken pox	Washing machine man coming
Measles	Ditto Telstra
Teething	Doctor
Up all night	Dentist
Car broken	Watch this space!

But it was a lot of fun. Be careful, though. Sometimes the stress caused by routine appointments is disproportionate to the pleasure gained when you actually get there.

TIME MARCHES ON

As children grow, the physical demands on us lessen and the mental demands increase. You must maintain the fitness level you have achieved through years of constant childcare, so now is the time to organise extracurricular exercise and perk up those dusting muscles.

Walk, swim, ride a bike, play tennis, ride a horse, mow the lawn, paint a ceiling, visit a gym, whatever, but do it you must.

Sorry!

WORKING MOTHERS

If your job entails strenuous physical exercise, such as nursing or digging potatoes, you do not need further exercise, so don't feel guilty. You are invariably exhausted all the time, as fit as a trout, have the stamina of ten men and would have survived the march across Singapore. And you would have got Bryan Brown.

If your work is sedentary, you will need to organise a fitness routine that doesn't include mothering or housework. Otherwise there is a risk of you turning nasty.

WHAT TO DO?

Sometimes it is difficult to know exactly what to do for exercise. There may be money restraints, weather problems, or the lurex gym job is festering in the bottom of the laundry basket. For me it was particularly hard as I don't like organised sports, women en masse, sweaty bodies, horses, being told what to do or treading in dog shit. I tried those home-workout videos but found the sexy instructors depressing in the extreme and, quite frankly, I didn't seem to be doing anything I hadn't done in bed the night before.

I thought about jogging, but I watched the locals trotting by and realised none of them ever smiled, so I gave the idea away. For two weeks I got excited about doing exercise and then went and lay down until the feeling passed.

No, I had to have something that was fun, easy, and would indulge my fantasies. So I developed the 'Maggie Groff One Hour Wacky Workout'.

THE MAGGIE GROFF ONE HOUR WACKY
WORKOUT—IT'S ABSOLUTELY FLABLESS

Every day I don swimmers and cap and climb into the pool, ocean or the indoor pool up the road if it's cold. I then perform the entire male lead role of *Riverdance* whilst mentally bonking Bryan Ferry. I can do it with or without music. I used to do *Swan Lake* but it wasn't as strenuous and I had a little trouble with the grands jetés. It is amazing to me how this clumsy, big-busted body of mine can prance elegantly about the pool. You can stand on your toes, yes you can, and do all those twisty fast leg movements, just like Michael Flatley. Naturally, it's better with the music, but it attracts too much attention if you are on the beach. And do you know, sometimes I even go into overtime. Sometimes I do it twice a day.

A word of warning. You will look a Proper Charlie doing this so wear a good camouflage swim cap and large sunglasses.

My apologies to Bryan Ferry.

CHAPTER NINE
TECHNO STRESS

Some days I look at my Baroness Deluxe Oven with the shiny knobs and rotisserie switches and scream, 'You bastard, why can't you just peel potatoes like I asked?' It's never replied. Not once. No doubt the manufacturers will come up with something soon. Meanwhile I'm gaga over gigabytes. Pin-numbered out. Laid waste by multi-tasking madness. Beep. Beep. Beep.

THE TELEPHONE
Telephones are surprisingly strong. I once threw mine out the back door and it hung in the evergreen alder for six hours. Time out for bad behaviour. I'm fair, though. If it's good I'll ring our favourite number. 'Hello,' I say. 'Is that the World's Greatest Hamburger Store?' 'No, sorry,' they reply, 'it's McDonald's!' It cracks us up every time.

My telephone's smart too. It knows when I'm glueing china, up a ladder, or secretly watching the midday movie. Years ago, it knew when I was smoking behind the garage.

The Home Office
Work from home? Don't let children answer the telephone. Ever. 'Hiya—yeah—'ang on' will damage sales figures. 'Mummy's having a drink' will shatter professional credibility. 'No, she's with the man next door' will destroy your reputation. Perception is everything.

You probably think I'm in a study, wearing literary person clothes. I'm not. I'm on the back steps, sporting a dressing gown and men's sports socks with cushion soles. See! Glad you can't . . .

Teensters
When young lerve takes hold, hours of drivel ooze down the lines. The receiver will smell of chips and cheap perfume called 'Intensity'. The language is Swahili. There is a lot of grunting.

Explain that the rest of the world pays a set quarterly fee for phone calls. Say something waffly about how wonderful it must be to make as many calls as you like. Then lower your lying eyes and add, 'Unfortunately, darling, in our street, the calls are charged individually.' I always think it's good to blame a major corporation when you can.

The Bill
Every three months those filthy piranhas from the telephone company try to savage our bank account. And every three months, Australiawide, men go ballistic over the bill. They have to. It's in the 'How To Be A Man Handbook'!

Mother's job is to protect and nurture her young. And herself. So, every three months, Australiawide, mothers hide telephone bills. In the same place they put school reports.

The Answering Machine
These are inexpensive, easy to operate, and your first line of defence against constant interruption. They annoy the hell out of:
- tele-marketing agents.
- relatives and other nuisance callers.
- teenagers who wish to be collected two hours earlier than planned.
- pale friendless virgins with personal problems.

Every mother should have an answering machine on staff. Sometimes, just for the heck of it, I say to my machine, 'Joan, take a letter.' I call it 'Joan' because people called Joan are extremely useful. I don't know why. They just are. So if you haven't got a Joan, get one pronto.

I'm waiting for the plumber while writing this. He's two hours late. No surprises there. When he arrives I'll give him a piece of my mind and refuse to pay the call-out fee. I'm sick and tired of tradesmen who think mothers have nothing to do all day but hang around waiting for them to come and save us. What a nerve. Oh! There he is now. Oh! Oh, my!

Quite the best-looking thing to walk up the driveway this year. I'd better put the kettle on. I wonder if he's had lunch . . .

Mobile Phonies

I expect if it was a hot day and I was on a desert road with a puncture and I'd just had my nails done and the last Mars bar had been eaten I'd quite like a mobile phone. For ordering pizza and stuff. You guessed! I don't have one. No use to me. You can't slam them down.

Most of my friends had one. Yes, had. Like the Spanish Civil War it seemed a good idea at the time. Mothers bleated safety concerns— school can contact you quickly in case of emergency blah blah blah. My friends received emergency calls—

'What's for dinner?'

'What are you doing now?'

'Where are my golf shoes?'

My friends switched off their mobile phones. My friends removed batteries from their mobile phones. My friends put their mobile phones at the back of their jewellery and belt drawers. RIP.

That was some plumber, let me tell you. I wonder what else I can break . . .

THE MICROWAVE

I don't have one of these, either. I've checked. Funny, I don't remember signing a hardship clause. I'm depressed now. I'll check the jewellery and belt drawer. Nope. Not there, either. But I did find an old letter to Santa which cheered me up no end.

A few years ago we had a microwave in a rental house. I used it to blow up potatoes. And one egg. It was good, too. Most artistic. By the time we moved I was exploding yams as well.

I'm adept at cleaning microwaves. I've had a lot of experience. Do you get the feeling I don't know much about microwaves? Many people swear by them. I swear at them. I'm often told they are good for heating babies' bottles. Here's some news. Babies don't need warm milk. Most of them don't miss a stroke if it's straight from the fridge.

If I were you I'd spend the money on a fabulous Le Creuset French Oven and a four dollar vegetable steamer from Woolies.

N.B. Le Creuset is expensive but you get what you pay for. They are handmade, enamelled cast iron, look impressive on the stove and have a lifetime guarantee. Many cooking shows use them. Watch out for specials—once a year they are heavily discounted. It's pronounced Le Crew-say.

A Techno Enigma

It's a funny old world, isn't it? My friend Gislaine, the Takeaway Queen of Tweed Heads, doesn't know how I cope without a microwave—I, who cook the full catastrophe every night, and then some. Gislaine is a qualified chef.

Then there's friend Bette, in the wilds of Papua New Guinea, making cakes on a tin plate over an open fire. Bette's a computer buff.

There's a moral in there somewhere. When you've worked it out, let me know.

THE DISHWASHER

For years I said, 'I don't need a dishwasher.' What a twit. Twit. Twit. Twit. In 1995 we bought a house with a gleaming new dishwasher. I fell in love. Even now, I polish the front and mouth 'thank you' as I pass by. The bending down and emptying lark are a bit of a pill but, you may have guessed, I've got my eye on the Fisher and Paykel two-drawer number. At last, technology for a mother ...

Tips

- Use regularly or it will smell.
- Use half the powder you are presently using.
- Unpack the bottom first. Empty the top, you're called away and, hey presto, someone's coffee dregs are dripping on the clean plates.
- Stack cutlery with spoons in one slot, forks in next, etc. This makes for easy unloading (obvious, but mothers are too tired for 'obvious').
- Check insurance policy. If the dishwasher leaks, you may find your household policy excludes floor coverings. Many do. You have to cover on contents insurance.

It's odd. I miss those wonderful evenings when my husband and I did the dishes together and chatted about family things. Oh ha ha.

THE TELEVISION

The world is full of stuffy old farts and child psychologists who think television is bad for children. They may be right, but Earth is no Utopia.

The baby is screaming, the phone is ringing, the car insurance was due two days ago, you're preparing dinner, you have a headache and someone aged four says, 'Can I watch telly?' Are you going to say, 'No, it's not on the pre-arranged viewing schedule'? Sucks boo to that.

The television is a valuable member of your staff. Like having another mother in the house when you need one. She is cheap to run, entertains for hours and you know the child is safe. It is beyond price if you are sick, the child is sick or you have something to do that doesn't require assistance.

What the child is watching is important. You know that. But be warned, the best intentions fly out the window when peer pressure takes hold. If you don't let them watch at home—they'll go to a friend's. Make rules if you want, but the world is against you, and rules are made to be broken. You heard it here first . . .

Advertising

Children aren't stupid. They see a toy doing fabulous things on television. They want one. They nail you to a wall and it's purchased for the birthday. The toy doesn't do fabulous things. It's just there. It's played with for two days. The box is played with for four. The child's been bitten. It won't forget.

Neither do you. Next time say, 'It's like the other ads, the toys aren't really doing it themselves. We'll go to a toy shop and you can see for yourself.'

You're on your own with the food ads.

Cable TV

We once spent a vacation on the Sunshine Coast. Me, the family, the remote control and Foxtel. I'm not saying any more.

THE VIDEO

I could write a book about what happens when we hire an overnight movie—I've never seen one the whole way through. I don't bother any more. I go to the cinema. People get thrown out for talking to you there.

Everything I've ever taped has been taped over. I can't tell you the language I use when I settle down to watch 'The Bill' and up pops a basketball game.

Videos, however, are extremely useful for entertaining youngsters, sleepovers, sickness and when people come to dinner who have particularly revolting offspring. Small children love to watch the same video over and over and over and over ... Tip: When you hire a children's video, ask the store to clean it—they often have muck on them and it will damage your tape heads.

THE COMPUTER

I'm not sure about this computer malarkey. It seems to me it takes a lot longer to check out at the library now than it ever did before. Do you remember those wonderful dog-eared card files they had? The smell reminded me of a book shop in Charing Cross Road. Mmmmm.

Not a day goes by without someone saying, 'Maggie, you need a computer.' No, I don't. What I need is a new wardrobe and a two-week cruise up the Ganges with every book on the bestseller list.

Besides, I've got a computer. Her name's Noela Pretty. But I call her 'Joan'.

HOW TO BREAK THE REMOTE CONTROL

The remote control stands alone. It has caused more wars than religion. It was invented by a man. I know it. I wouldn't be surprised to see one cited in a divorce case.

Men drive them. Forwards, backwards, stop, go, pause, switch to the sport. It's an addiction. Don't seize the remote in a rage and jump on it. You were born with cunning. Use it.

Methodology

Remove batteries and replace with duds. Do this two or three times until 'others' get frustrated. Next you bend the silver plates at the end of the battery compartment to make a bigger space for the battery. The connection is now loose. What a shame. Sometimes it works, sometimes it doesn't. 'Others' are getting very annoyed. Some have learned to walk again. Time for total destruction.

The casing on a remote control is brittle and cracks easily. How lucky can you get? The simplest method is to position the control at an angle sticking out of a drawer. Slam the drawer shut. Darn. You've broken it. Off to the repairers. Lose the receipt.

THE APPLIANCE CUPBOARD

Give me strength. Who thought this one up? Rows of gourmet gizmos plugged at the ready. I've never cooked in a cupboard. Does cooking in a kitchen the size of a cupboard count?

SUMMING UP

You have gathered I do not consider modern technology conducive to happy families. At the moment it controls us, not the other way around. Think hard. Are you in the driver's seat? Is it saving time and effort? Or is it causing stress and costing money?

But, then, what do I know? I didn't want an upside down fridge because I was worried about milk spilling everywhere . . .

BACK TO BASICS

Time for a sensible treat. Today you are going to buy a dozen teaspoons—mothers never have enough. Put them in the broken mug you can't bear to throw out and stand next to the kettle. Isn't this more useful than a computer?

HELLO MARKETING

Would someone please produce a functional cutlery set. Mothers need:

10 steak knives   6 serving spoons
10 knives   20 teaspoons
10 butter knives   2 children's knives
10 big forks   2 children's forks
10 dessert forks   2 baby spoons
10 dessert spoons   2 sets salad servers
10 soup spoons

Matching please. And, while you're at it, you can fix the sheet set nonsense. We want sets of fitted sheet, quilt cover (or flat sheet) and *four* pillowcases for big beds and fitted sheet, quilt cover (or flat sheet) and *two* pillowcases for singles.

WWW.sothere.com.au

CHAPTER TEN
SLEEP—ZZZZZ

I'm something of an expert on sleep, lack of it, anyway. I blame heredity. My father, like Winston Churchill, only needed a few hours a night. Me too. My mother and brother slept like logs. No, like forests. Guess what I got? Yes. I got Pavarotti. On the hour, every hour. For two years and eleven days.

I used to get wildly excited by books full of sleep tips for babies, and when the sun's right, I can still see the dent in the wall where I threw one of them. A book, not a baby. Nothing worked. It was me against the Mississippi. Sometimes I just called her 'Issippi' and left off the 'Miss' part. There's no need to be formal at 2 a.m.

You see, for some of us, sleep ceases the moment we give birth, and recommences when the dog dies and the children leave home. What happens in between is called Nappus Interruptus. And in the immortal words of my mother, she of immense style, 'You just have to bloody well get on with it.'

BABIES—GORGEOUS BABIES
It's a jolly good job that little babies are so utterly scrumptious you can't help loving them to bits. Yes, siree. A jolly, jolly good job . . . I

was told new babies sleep 20 out of 24 hours. Where are these babies? I want one.

BO-BOS FOR BA-BIES
Getting a tiny baby off to sleep is like completing an application form for NASA. It can be very difficult.
- If the baby falls asleep while feeding, don't jerk them upright for a burping session. Lay them down and skidaddle.
- Babies stay awake more each day as they get older. They can't actually do anything, so wake time will involve being cooed at and cuddled, or lying in their cot staring at 4000 things you have stuck on the ceiling. Many drift off to sleep this way.
- Some babies lie in their cots and grizzle in a half-hearted fashion. Let them get on with it. Drop to the floor and crawl out of the room.

So what do you do with 20-odd inches of screaming clench-fisted fury? Especially if you have a dreamboat that vomits if left to cry. You don't care if the baby is asleep or not. It's crying that drives you up the wall and, quite frankly, you'd agree to marry Homer Simpson if it would shut your baby up.

WHY BABIES CRY

Hunger	Frightened
Cold/Hot	Want Mummy/Daddy
Wet/Nappy Rash	Bored
Sick	Over-tired

WHAT TO DO
- Check the nappy.
- If you think they are still hungry, give 20–30 ml of cooled boiled water from a bottle.

- Pick one of the following systems and, if it works, stick to it until it bleeds. Ignore free advice that you are making a rod for your own back, because if it works, you have won.

System One

Pick up and cuddle. Most babies settle when held upright with their head nestled in mum's neck. This ensures she won't be able to do anything else. Walk around, sing, and pat them on the nappy area gently. Allow ten minutes after you think they have fallen asleep— they are tricky little devils. Lay them down and continue singing and patting until you are certain they have nodded off.

System Two

Lay the baby in a pram or stroller, tuck them in and go for a walk. Around the house if it's nighttime. Motion will send a baby off to sleep. Don't transfer them to a cot.

System Three

Lay them in the cot. Sit down and sing and pat the nappy area. If screams change to grizzle, get up and start tidying the room, occasionally giving a reassuring pat. Then creep out.

System Four—For the Desperadoes

Put them in the car and go for a drive. Share your baby.

Quite often, the whole performance can take three hours, by which time the baby needs feeding again. This is why new mothers say, 'I never get anything done' and 'I don't remember'.

I have to tell you, it's been unbridled adventure at No 54 today. We had a King Brown snake in the garden. We get a lot of snakes, pretty green tree jobs and large carpet designs. I wouldn't be a bit surprised if David Attenborough wasn't hiding in the bushes.

Poor King B. had to go. Flopsy Bunny said so. Sorry, I forgot to mention I speak 'Rabbit'. Anyway, I called Roger, the snake catcher who, unfortunately, was nothing like the plumber. He turned up in shorts, thongs and dark glasses. I had expected high-powered rifles and thigh-level boots. All Roger had was a packet of Benson and Hedges and a hessian bag. This was a major disappointment. Like Roger.

I would like to say there was much danger and thrashing about. It took Roger two minutes to pick up the snake and bag it, and 20 minutes for him to help me down from the Hills Hoist.

Roger said it was a harmless tree snake. What does he know? I paid him $30. Then I phoned my husband and told him it was a taipan.

SLEEPING THROUGH

To those who have babies that 'sleep through', this means 11.30 p.m. to 4 a.m. To those who have babies that don't sleep through, in, over, under or beside anything, they think this means 7 p.m. to 7 a.m.

So shut up about your sleeping through business. It's a terminological inexactitude. That means a lie. Mothers shouldn't tell lies. At least, not silly ones like this. Because you've been caught.

NEIGHBOURS

Naturally, being such a nice person, I worried about waking the neighbours. Unfortunately we had a psychiatrist one side, a childless frowning couple the other and an over-sexed cook upstairs who was tap-dancing her way to alienation with the lads from the submarine base down the road. Top that!

FACTS AND FOIBLES
- A crying baby sounds louder to you than to others.
- Neighbours only get upset if a crying baby is unattended.
- Give an occasional peace offering. A bottle of plonk goes a long way.
- Given birth to the Glenn Miller Band? Put heavy curtains, a rug, more furniture, cushions and a pile of towels in the room to absorb volume.

000

A crying baby is not an emergency. A broken corkscrew—now that's an emergency. You are not the cavalry. Get off your horse and learn to amble. Practise. Go on. Get up now and amble to the other end of the house and back.

ROUTINE

Yes, let's hear it for good old routine. BOOOOOOO. BOOOOOOO. Routine is for single mothers with no other children who live alone in a one-room shack on a desert island in the middle of an Alaskan lake. Without a phone. Nice idea, though, fellas. Nice idea. For most mothers with a new baby, the fact that Wednesday and Thursday follow Monday and Tuesday is as close to routine as they'll get.

DADDY

(Oh no—we haven't forgotten him.) Imagine this. It's a dark and stormy night. You're three months old. Cold and hungry. Which would you prefer?

a) A soft-edged pinky vision with warm milky curves;
b) A naked man with rough scratchy skin who's using the 'F' word a lot?

Just asking . . .

HOW TO GET BACK TO SLEEP AFTER A NIGHTTIME FEED

(When woken by a baby, not after utilising answer b.)

- Easier if the baby is beside you as you won't be actively over-stimulated.
- Don't speak. One word can break the somnolent spell.
- Ignore nonsense about cocoa in a thermos flask.
- Leave classical music to cows in milking sheds.

- If you want, feed the baby in bed with you. I must say, waking in the morning with a baby in your arms is like nothing on earth. You should try it just once. It's wild.

Sometimes, if you sleep with your baby, both sleep rhythms synchronise—the deep together and the light together. Often you wake first. It's magic. Mother Nature in action.

HELP
This is where you want to get hit by that truck I was talking about in chapter one. You need a day in bed. Here's how to do it.
- Call in all favours.
- Ask a friend or relative for help during the day.
- Feed the baby and hand them over to the helper. Tell them to go out for at least three hours.
- Put in earplugs and go to bed. Don't touch the housework.
- When you wake, feed the baby again and hand them back.
- Go back to bed for another three hours.

A day's help is the best gift anyone can give a new mother.

HOW TO MAKE A COUPON BOOK
This is the ideal gift for workmates to prepare. Each person writes their gift on a small sheet of paper. Suggestions:
- Three hours free babysitting on a Saturday night.
- One load of ironing.
- A day's help at home.
- One mow of the lawn.
- A free trip to the hairdresser.

Staple the coupons together and make a fancy front cover. It beats six rattles and four balls hands down.

WHERE IS THE BABY?

Not long after intercoms came on the market I noticed modern houses developed an unusual floor plan. The Main Bedroom became the Parents' Retreat, located two kilometres from children's rooms. It's call the 'Us and Them' layout. It comes with a bicycle for mother.

Your baby should be exactly where you want them to be. In bed with you, next to you in a bassinet or in a room close by. And you don't need an intercom. Mothers can hear their baby the other side of a pig shed.

MUSICAL BEDS

This is fun. Players start off in their own beds. By morning, dad is in the four-year-old's room and mum, the baby and the seven-year-old are in the parental bed. The four-year-old is in the baby's cot. The dog is in the seven-year-old's bed.

And the little one said, 'Roll over, roll over . . .'

DOWN THE TRACK

When your baby is about six months old you can start to be firm about sleep. Right on. Go to your room. And while you're at it, change your nappy.

Believe me I was firm. But me and the Mississippi, we just kept on banking and weaving through pastures and meadows until that glorious day, at the age of two, when the flood quelled and the mighty waters receded.

Then I couldn't sleep because I thought she was dead.

THE CONTROLLED CRYING TECHNIQUE

This is for babies over six months. It teaches them to go back to sleep on their own when they wake at night. It involves letting the baby cry for a few minutes before giving basic comfort, such as a pat. You leave as soon as cries change to whimpers. Now let them cry for five minutes, then return and repeat basic comfort, but leave as soon as screams subside. Repeat in increments of a few minutes until a ten-minute maximum. You must be consistent for success.

I failed. I cried. I vomited. It was the most stressful thing I've ever done. Nature had not equipped me to go against my instincts. And I can't fight nature. Or the phone company.

RUMPY PUMPY

A brief word about sex. The most important sex organ in the human body is the brain. It is difficult to feel sexy and attractive when your nether regions have been ripped to shreds, hormones are bouncing around the universe, huge leaky breasts look like road maps and you still have the turning circle of the QE2.

So listen up, my pretties. It matters not that old man Yates, the seed supplier, is behaving as if he's on the FBI's ten most romantic list, and that coitus, when attempted, is akin to forcing a marshmallow in a piggy bank.

Fear not. Like General MacArthur, desire will return. Until it does I suggest you read up on the antechinus, a little-known native Australian animal. The male drops dead from exertion after mating. It's a good read at the right time.

Personally speaking I would have been quite happy if the doctor had said, 'You shouldn't resume marital relations for four to six months, Mrs Groff.'

WORKING MOTHERS

Unfortunately babies don't always arrive when planned. Mortgages, expensive real estate and prior work commitments mean that many women have to return to the paid workforce soon after the birth.

There is no way they can do both jobs properly. It's not possible. For anyone. Many try the controlled crying technique so they can sleep. It may work for a short while but, be prepared, teething, sickness, nightmares, visitors, holidays and things that go bump in the night will mean you are frequently starting over again. And children who spend a lot of time in childcare get sick quite often.

Want to go back to work? Think you can do it all? Worried about intellectual stimulation? Scared you'll be bored? Ho hum. There are few careers that can't be put on hold for a couple of years. If nothing else, think of your health. You'll definitely be thinking of sleep. A lot.

TAKING A NAP

What a joke. How many times was I told to lie down every time the child slept? Right. And let the staff get on with their chores.

I remember planning a nap. It was 1989. A wet and windy day. No visitors. No appointments. Answering machine on. Note on the door saying I was a lapsed member of two religions. Child asleep.

I lay down. A magpie flew into the window. Smack. Shatter. Plop. I spent the afternoon burying wildlife and phoning glass companies.

BEDTIME

You can lead a horse to water but you can't make it sleep. You know what I mean. Children need rest and sleep. They need a seven o'clock deadline.

If children don't sleep well they:
- are bad-tempered.
- are unable to concentrate at school.
- their immune system falters and they get sick.

Establish a routine and stick to it. Like glue. Toilet, bath, teeth, story, bed and a large brandy for you. Leave the light on if they want, give them a book, but your job is done. Bottoms up!

In some homes it's fashionable to keep children up so they can play with mum or dad when they get home from work. I think daddy should be playing with mummy and vice-versa. Tired parents and tired children is a recipe for disaster.

HANDS OFF COCKS. HANDS ON SOCKS

If you think the transport arrangements for the Olympic Games are a nightmare you should spend a morning in my house. Actually, no you shouldn't. You'd be trampled to death.

I'd like to know what dimwit decided that by the age of seven children can dress themselves, tie shoes, clean teeth and brush hair. They can't even do it at sixteen. Heavens. You can't even wake them at sixteen. I remember my mother storming through our bedrooms screaming, 'Higher primate coming through', while she seized the covers from our beds. You'd have liked her. No one could touch her for innovative procedures.

It's a sad fact, but the only thing that's bright-eyed and bushy-tailed and ready for breakfast in our home is the rabbit. And me. Sort of. I don't get the breakfast part.

Today I'm going to buy a trumpet.

CHAPTER ELEVEN
SCHOOL

It's 6 a.m. The sun, like everyone in Banora Point, is on time today. Wagtails curve and glide from palm to poinciana, waterdragons stand sentinel on garden walls, wild ducks dive and surprise pool reflections and retired folk tug yorky and silky in arthritic procession along the road. God's creatures. And every last one of them has crapped on our front lawn. Well, perhaps not the retired folk ...

You'd better fetch a thermos of calming beverage because this is a big chapter. I don't know about you, but school interfered with my education. I lived only for clothes, tennis and the holidays. And Graham Walker in Year 11.

I need laughter. Here we go. An oldie, but a goodie.

MOTHER:	Son, get up—it's late!
SON:	I want to stay in bed.
MOTHER (loudly):	Get up now! It's time to go to school.
SON:	But I don't want to go to school.
MOTHER (very loudly):	Get up and go to school. You have to go. You're the principal.

PRE-SCHOOL

Pre-school is a clever title for childcare, the name inferring it will prepare children for school. Watch out! It'll be Toilet Training College next. (Now, there's an idea!) Good grief, at three my daughter was Wind Whistler pony, neighing about the garden and eating oats from a bowl on the path. She needed educating like she needed anthrax.

KINDERGARTEN

The first year of school is called 'kindergarten'. Translated it's 'children's garden'. You can't fail children's garden. Come top. Or bottom.

It's great fun—story-telling, make-believe, counting, singing, reading, building, painting, learning through creative play and occasionally wetting your pants. Wonderful stuff—a smooth transition for children, a nightmare for the teacher and heaven for little old you.

THE NATIONAL ANTHEM

Have you ever listened to the words young children sing:

> *'Australians all love ostriches,*
> *Four minus one is three . . .'*

I fell about laughing so much I missed the rest.

READY TEDDY GO

Yes, you can put away those brochures on freelance work in the Middle East—salvation may be at hand. The benchmark for school readiness is social confidence and emotional development. Whatever that means. Sounds a bit hit and miss to me. Let's pretend it means:

- They are of eligible age.
- They want to go and you think they are ready.
- You want them to go and they think they are ready.
- You work and can't afford childcare. Then it's best foot forward Sonny Jim and social confidence be blowed.
- Your child's friends are starting.

And for heaven's sake, if you've made a mistake, take them out.

I know! Let's have babies in September. Then all children would start school at five and a half. Perfect. Think what it'd do for obstetricians' golf days.

WHICH SCHOOL?
The one whose uniform doesn't need ironing.

Something You Need to Know
It is in a school's interest to present itself as the best. They do this to keep numbers up and ensure staff jobs. This is why the day before Kindergarten Open Day, you see computers and pianos wheeled into classrooms . . .

Something Else You Need to Know
The most important thing in any school is the teacher. Not mahogany desks and whizzbang technology, not enormous school halls or fertile playing fields, it's plain old Miss Watson with the high-pitched singing voice and the gnarled pointy finger.

Private vs Public
Don't imagine private schools have better teachers than the state system. It's possible Mr Turps in Year 8 at the private establishment has a degree in statistics and is teaching maths, while Mrs Frobisher of 7F at the local state has a four-year degree in education majoring in maths with twenty-five years experience.

The greater advantage of private schools is discipline—they can throw out unruly children, ensuring a good learning environment. In state schools, children throw the teachers, and all they get is counselling.

THE FIRST DAY
It's etched in my brain. Next to first stitches and first fillings.

I grew up in a house where people came and went with the tides.

Grown-ups talked of storms in Bilbao, cargo in Valparaiso and the vagaries of the Suez Canal. I talked to my father in the Atlantic on a ship-to-shore radio and listened to jungle tales of rubber-planting grandparents in Malaya. Imagine my excitement when at last, I, Maggie, was going somewhere. Even if it was Castle Street County Primary at the end of town.

And so I was launched into the school system, with a few stern words, Bible-black shoes and a five-mile walk home. Indulgence and pampering were forbidden. Adversity bred fortitude and good character.

Then I met Charlie Bushell, aged five. He tied me to the school fountain with my skipping rope and told me Reggie Two-Sticks, the wicked old man who lived on a boat at Portchester Castle, would come and eat me.

Here endeth the first lesson . . .

BEFORE D-DAY

- Don't harp on about starting school. Less said the best.
- Practise opening lunchbox and drink bottle. Very funny. Them, not you.
- Attend Kindergarten Orientation Day.
- Register at school, check starting date and uniform requirements.
- Are immunisations up to date?
- Check there isn't a boy called Charlie Bushell starting too.

D-DAY

- Allow an extra half-hour to get ready.
- Ignore tantrums. Let everything go this morning. Just be your usual calm pleasant self!?
- Don't worry if the child can't eat breakfast today. It doesn't matter.
- Make a packed lunch the child is familiar with.
- Let them take a toy—put name on it.

- Take child to school yourself and stay until the teacher tells you to go.
- Show the child where you will be standing at the end of the day.
- Be guided by the teacher. If the child is screaming and the teacher says go—then go.
- Don't stare at other mothers having a bad time. Oh, okay. Just a bit then.
- Cry all the way home.

UNIFORMS

As 'mother' you will be on first name terms with the lost-property bin. Buy a black permanent laundry marker from the newsagent and label everything, even shoes. And what sparky thought of short white socks? Let me at 'em.

Tips

- Don't knit a beautiful jumper—it will be used to hang from parallel bars.
- Avail yourself of the uniform shop.
- A zip in a pocket keeps money safe.
- Individualise school bag with a badge or ribbon—otherwise they'll come home with the wrong one.
- Uniforms are put on after breakfast.
- Don't buy three new sets of everything before Day One. Great uniforms are returned to the uniform shop in the first week of school.

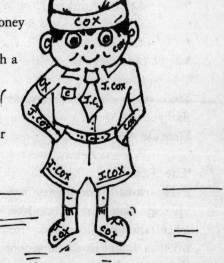

- Don't buy cheap tights for girls. Expensive ones are tougher and look fine with a few mends. They are warmer, wash well, and cheaper in the long run. N.B. Tights often come home a bit damp—this is normal in the early years as tights are very hard to get off if you're in a hurry. Still are!

THE SCHOOL GATES

Psst. Psst. Psst. Mothers gossip ... Take it from me, the teacher is a wonderful scapegoat for a child's inadequacies. So don't listen to tittle-tattle. It will cause unnecessary anguish.

For the most part you have a symbiotic relationship with parents of your child's school friends. You use them. They use you. A necessary evil. Sometimes you find firm friends, but don't get excited—your spouses won't get on. It must be in that darned 'How To Be A Man Handbook'.

You Need to Know

- Where they live/phone number?
- Do they drive?
- Do they have a ferocious doberman/breed pit bulls?
- Do they drink? (You don't want a closet alcy driving your child. There are a few around so be careful.)
- Do they work? (Can they reciprocate with after-school play?)
- Are they always late?

Mothers come in all shapes and sizes. Some will astound you, and you find yourself secretly wondering how their child ever got to be five ... Here are two of my favourites:

The Tart

Every school has one. They have wild flowing hair and so much make-up they look like an accident in a paint factory. They stand close when talking, voices husky from two packs of Marlboro a day. They smell of mints in the afternoon to smother a liquid lunch. Even on the coldest day their clothing is arranged to expose glimpses of breast.

Don't be fooled. These mothers are fun and can get a male principal or caretaker to do anything they ask. And they have great wig collections for the school play.

The Corporate Pain in the Petunia

You spot these at school functions. They wear suits and very high heels. They have mobile phones and umbrellas with BMW printed on them. They ring and ask you to pick up their child from school because they are in a meeting (a euphemism for 'I've got a leg over the boss') and they are always late. They work one day a term in the school canteen. This is so they can bore the pants off you with how important they are, then bore the pants off the corporate world with the caring-mother routine. I usually tell them, when asked, that I'm a helicopter pilot with air-sea rescue. Trouble is, they rarely ask.

EXCUSE NOTES

Dear Miss Spicer

The dishwasher flooded and I didn't have a clean uniform for Harry because we had people to dinner last night and they brought their naughty son Damian who wouldn't go to sleep so poor defenceless Harry couldn't sleep either and he doesn't feel well today and he's under the doctor.

Yours faithfully
Felicity Watson.

I think poor Felicity got sozzled. What do you think?

I wonder if teachers sit around staffrooms and read these out for a laugh. I hope so.

The Department of Education needs to know when and why your child was absent. This is so they can set the rozzers on you if they have too much time off.

An Excuse Note Should Contain

- Your child's name.
- The class.
- Date of absence.
- Reason for absence. 'John was unwell' will suffice.
- If the child had an infectious disease, note this as well.
- Your signature.
- Address it to the class teacher.

Example

12 August 1998

Dear Miss Spicer

Harry Watson of 4G was absent from school on 10 August 1998. He was unwell.

Regards
Felicity Watson.

PACKED LUNCHES
(Facilitus makus. Facilitus ditchus.)
When I was a child, school served a hot meal at lunchtime. We sat at tables of eight, first or second sitting, and devoured such delicacies as toad in the hole, shepherd's pie and various vegetables stewed to hell and gone. Desserts were pink and wobbly. To this day I gag at the smell of boiled swede or the sight of a throbbing mass on a pudding plate.

Where is the Chicken?
Preparing lunches every day can take on the dimensions of climbing Everest without Sherpa Tensing. Sure as eggs someone has eaten the chicken you were saving, carrots and alfalfa were pillaged by livestock, bran muffins went off to camp and tadpoles are floating in the lunchbox. And you're already 20 minutes late . . .

The Reality
Here is a sample of what happens to a packed lunch:
- It will be eaten before morning bell.
- Lunchbox will come home unopened.
- Contents are removed from wrappers, bruised and uneaten.
- Your homemade muesli slice traded for chips.
- Contents untouched but box now contains leaves and grated rubber from play equipment.
- Contents untouched. Milky Way wrappers in child's pocket.
- Lunchbox empty but child is starving. (???)
- Lunchbox contains remains of someone else's sandwich.
- Lunchbox does not come home.

A variation of the above may happen daily for three years. If it doesn't there is something wrong with your child. Or you have given birth to Robert Carrier.

The Worry
Because mothers are indomitable, and it is the nature of the beast to override insurmountable challenges life throws at us, like uneaten lunch, you will continue to pack basic, familiar fare and not succumb to idealistic nonsense and prepare outrageously time-consuming gourmet delicacies in the hope they will be eaten. If you do, hypertension is your reward.

Ensure your child has a healthy breakfast and a sensible dinner and feed the hard dry remains from the lunchbox to next door's labrador. Now, if the child gets rickets at age ten, it will not be your fault.

Some Simple Rules
- Butter sandwiches and rolls. Otherwise fillings fall out.
- Cut things in easily held chunks.
- Wrap food in paper sandwich bags or greaseproof. Small containers will be lost.
- Cutlery will be lost.
- If child likes vegemite sandwiches, make them every day.
- Teach child to use water bubblers.

- Tell child to put used wrappers, apple cores etc. back in lunchbox—you can see what they've eaten.

Here is a good thing to do. During kindergarten year you can help children at lunchtime—open boxes and drinks, encourage nourishment and assist the teacher to keep them sitting down. What a nice person I am to think of this. You may even get a bite of teacher's valium sandwich ...

And don't forget, as soon as your child is capable, they should be making lunch themselves. Let's say, for argument's sake, about age 24.

Things to Avoid
- Unfamiliar food.
- Stainers—beetroot, plums.
- Foods that make you heave while preparing them.
- Fruits that bruise—pears, tomatoes.
- Things that are difficult to hold—guinea pigs. Just joking.
- Pure juice if it gives child headaches (orange juice can do this).

- Chips—they have no place in a regular diet.
- Chocolate. This is currency, not lunch.
- In hot weather, bananas and milk products.
- Designer food. No school child is going to eat tofu.

Treats

It will be reported back on day one that *all* other children had chips and chocolate for lunch. And their mother let them buy an ice-block from the canteen. Oh really? Nice try. Beware—a kindergarten child with a regular lunchbox of delicious booty is a sitting duck for older children with no conscience. Save treats for birthdays.

The Food—At Last

A lunchbox should contain four basic things:
- Something for little lunch.
- A drink.
- Two things for big lunch.

At least one item should be fruit or raw vegetables.

At least one item should involve bread or similar product.

LIST ONE

NATURAL FOODS—
CHOOSE ONE ITEM FROM THIS LIST

Photocopy these lists and stick on kitchen cupboard.

I use the term 'natural foods' with a certain amount of licence. Many breads contain preservatives but, for our purposes here, we shall not be lunchbox Gestapo.
- Mini pizza—spread tomato paste thinly on small pita or pocket bread. Sprinkle with parmesan and grill. Wrap in foil.
- Slice of homemade quiche.
- Sandwiches—cold meat
  - —egg (this falls out!)
  - —cheese and vegemite
  - —cheese
  - —vegemite

—tuna
—peanut butter
—cucumber
—cottage cheese
—lettuce and cucumber
—smoked mussels and sun-dried tomato (Gotcha!)

Remember, keep it simple. You don't need to be grating carrot at 7 a.m.

LIST TWO
NATURAL FOODS—
CHOOSE TWO ITEMS FROM THIS LIST

Apple

Peach

Nectarine

Homemade popcorn (cook a lot and store)

Mandarin

Grapes

Orange (peeled and in plastic bag)

Kiwi fruit (cut in half, scoop out and replace in skin)

Box of sultanas

Banana

Cracker sandwich with butter and vegemite

Hard-boiled egg (peeled)

Pikelet sandwich with butter

Pretzels—baked wheat thins

Strawberries (leave husks on)

Slice of fruit loaf

Sliced carrot, celery, broccoli or cauliflower florets

Dates

Buttered scone

Mini unprocessed cheeses with crackers

Melon (skin off in hand-size chunks)

Bread and butter sandwich (some children like two sandwiches)

Yoghurt (say bye-bye to the plastic spoon)

Prepacked natural fruit (available in small tins with peel-off lid)

Yoghurt sultanas (from health food stores)
Homemade slice or cookies
Cherry tomatoes
Celery sticks filled with peanut butter
Chicken leg wrapped in foil
Sliced green pepper, carrot or cucumber (in plastic sandwich bag)

LIST THREE
ALMOST NATURAL FOODS

Dried apples
Dried apricots
Pre-packed muesli bars
Pre-packed fruit slices
Cooked sausage (wrapped in foil) (Buy lots, freeze in pairs)
Pre-packed cheese and cracker snacks
Small packs of flavoured crackers
Salami sticks (available from deli)
Cheese sticks

TIRED DAYS

This is the five-year-old's guide to a nine-day fortnight. It's a bad idea and probably against the law. I just thought, you know, I'd run it past you. So you can see what a good thing it isn't.

It wasn't pioneered by my friend, Bambi, in Melbourne in the early 80s. I thought it was such a bad idea I didn't continue it at Neutral Bay Public School in Sydney.

I understand it involves keeping a tired kindergarten child home about one day every two weeks for a rest and a play with mother. That's 20 tired days a year. Yes, it certainly sounds dreadful. I'm glad I didn't do it.

THE TEACHER

I had a teacher called Miss Parker Bowles. Now there's a thing! We called her 'Pooky Bowels'. This is frightfully funny when you're only twelve . . .

Actually, it's not bad when you're 45.

Good Mauling Miss Pooky Bowels.

Couldn't resist.

Firstly, I'd like to apologise to teachers for the appalling way you are treated by the media, politicians, the Education Department, parents and students. I'm so sorry.

Teachers are professionals. They teach. They do not clean classrooms, mediate in custody battles, pick up litter, feed children lunch or become social workers between 9 a.m. and 3 p.m.

TROUBLESHOOTING

So the heir apparent has blotted his copy book. Only one thing to remember. Children lie. GREAT BIG PORKIES.

No child is going to admit to their parents they were rude or misbehaved. It's a bit like everyone in jail being innocent. The child has had all day to think up a much better story—usually embellished with 'Maria Ferguson's father wrote a letter of complaint to the Principal about Miss Nesbitt.'

Don't fire off a letter. Talk to the teacher. Politely!

WHAT YOU SHOULD TELL THE TEACHER

If home situation has changed, i.e. divorce, separation, death, moving house, a dead pet, sibling to university, new baby. All these have a dramatic effect on a child's behaviour.

WHAT YOUR CHILD WILL TELL THE TEACHER

Oh, just about every personal secret your family has. Miss Clarke will know you drank too much on Friday night and daddy used the 'f word on the phone and cousin Mary has 'a problem'.

Once, when asked what her father was, my daughter answered, 'He's a mental retard.' I can't imagine where she got this from. Okay. If I think real hard it'll come to me . . .

AT YEAR'S END

A note of appreciation will mean a lot. Sending it via the principal is a nice touch. A bottle of wine or chocolates won't be knocked back either. (Don't send this via the principal!) The best gift ever was when all the mothers bought a Christmas ornament for the teacher's tree. She'd just got married so, I guess, in the decoration department she was set for life.

THE CANTEEN

School canteen is the largest takeaway food chain in the country. Profit goes to the school. There isn't much profit in salad, bananas and apples so, over time, sausage rolls and their relatives have crept into the warming oven.

Some schools are 'healthy'. Power to them—school is exactly where children should be shown good nutrition. Unfortunately many are still chasing the processed pie dollar.

Helping in the canteen is a great learning experience. You get the latest on who is bonking Almandine Beckwith-Flint's mother, a current update on divorce settlements, the best hairdresser and who Miss Mason was with at the cinema on Friday. It's 'Neighbours' on stage.

HELPING AT SCHOOL

This will tell you more about your child's abilities than a school report.

My first time was for reading. I took a group of four kindergarten children into the playground and we sat on a bench under a tree and I read to them, and then they had a go. At least, that was what was supposed to happen.

All four children had Saint Vitus's dance. They did everything to the bench but sit on it. By the end of page one there were only three children. I couldn't see Kazu anywhere. I told the others to sit still while I searched. One of them promptly fell backwards off the bench and howled. I can still see Mrs Edwards's face grinning at me through the classroom window as she pointed into the tree.

I left Kazu up there and suffered in silence as he dropped gumnuts on my head while I read to the remnants. I tell you, I wouldn't be a teacher for quids.

I got better as years went by. I graduated to embroidery and second-place ribbon holder on sports day. The pinnacle of my career will be to fire the starting gun. At Kazu.

THERE AND BACK AGAIN
Bus
Great friendships are established on buses. Enemies too. And every child hates the driver. I can't imagine, not for a single minute, why school bus drivers get cranky. First time on the homeward run is nerveracking—will they get the right stop? Did they get on? It's worse than having teeth pulled. For a week I drove to school, put my daughter on the bus with a friend then drove to our bus stop. Am I crazy or am I crazy? No. Just your average mother . . .

Walk
Depends how far really. A policeman told me children under 12 shouldn't be crossing roads alone. This crossing lark is a bone of contention between parents and causes minor skirmishes. Err on the side of caution—which, incidentally, is your side.

Car
Observe parking signs outside school. About once a year police fine miscreants to clear congestion—usually in March. I wonder what would happen if the School Parents and Citizens Association (P and C) handed out Doctor on Call stickers . . .

EXTRA CLASSES
Teachers are harangued by disgruntled parents when they suggest a child is struggling in certain areas. 'I want them moved' and 'She's not doing her job properly' are two favoured parental phrases. Wake

up! It shows the teacher is on the ball, and gives you a chance to address the problem with extra classes or help at home. Better to find out now than next year.

HOMEWORK

I remember cringing in horror at a kindergarten parent night when a frosty father asked Miss Warren why there was no homework.

Miss Warren shone brilliantly. 'Oh, Mr Muldoon,' she said in her shaky happy voice, 'I think Joshua can wait another year or two for homework. At least until he's killed all those pirates in your back garden.'

Says it all really, doesn't it?

Nonsense

A special desk and special chair in a special spot will not encourage one child to do one night's homework. Children need to do it anywhere.

- On a moving bus.
- In the back seat of a car parked outside Woolworths.
- At the doctor's surgery.
- At grandma's dining room table.
- In the kitchen, close to assistance.
- On the floor beside your desk at work.

Welcome to Homework Reality.

Things You Need to Know

- First time homework knocks children sideways. Expect nightmares.
- In the early years you should help—it's a barometer of the child's progress.
- In high school you need to know what they have to do and *when it has to be done by.* Then you have to remind them every day. For six years.
- How to forge your child's handwriting!

Mother's Little Homework Helper

A NOUN   is the name of anything as *school* or *garden*, *hoop* or *swing*.

A PRONOUN   stands instead of a noun as *she* instead of Brenda Brown.

A VERB   tells us of anything done as *jump* or *skip* or *fly* or *run*.

An ADVERB   tells *how*, *why*, *when* or *where* as he travelled *behind* and she sat *there*.

An ADJECTIVE   describes the noun as *pretty* flowers or *clever* scribes.

A PREPOSITION   stands before the noun, as *in* or *through* the door.

CONJUNCTIONS   join the words together as men *and* women, wind *or* weather.

INTERJECTION   shows surprise as *Oh!* how pretty. *Ah!* how wise.

Author unknown.

COMPOSITE CLASSES

I thought this referred to classrooms. You know, brick and tile, wood and plaster. I couldn't understand why it was important.

A composite class is a mixture of children from two or more year levels of schooling. The old one-room schoolhouse is a classic example. It's formed when there are too many or too few children from one year to make up a complete class, so they are amalgamated with one of the year levels either side.

Children continue to follow the curriculum for their normal year of schooling. They are not being 'kept down' or 'put up', although it's interesting that you never hear parents of children combined with the year ahead complain.

BUDDY SYSTEM/PEER SUPPORT GROUP

When I was at school we used the Buddy System during swimming lessons. If the whistle blew you had to find your buddy and clasp hands in the air. If you remained alone, one of you was dead.

The Buddy and Peer Support Systems encourage respect and familiarity between age groups, in direct contrast to the 'Just tread on her, she's only a kindy' attitude.

Peer Support Group

Formed at the beginning of a school year, it constitutes five or six children, one from each year. Members are called 'buddies'. They assist each other in the playground, at school functions and outings.

Buddy System

This pairs two children from the school, usually a youngest and eldest. It's brilliant on both sides—gives security to one and responsibility to the other. And great peace of mind to mother.

EDUCATION SPEAK

This will help decipher an official blurb from Head Office.

Simulated behavioural feedback: Returning Robert's disgusting drawing.

Responsive performance models: Gym equipment.

Adaptive organisational environment: Demountable classrooms.

Diagnostic learning systems: Tests.

Interactive instructional monitoring: Teaching.

Diagnostic student accountability: Who did this?

Computer-based performance evaluation: Reports.

Individualised teaching feedback: Homework.

Differentiated contingency monitoring: Is everyone here?

Multi-dimensional behavioural management: Punishment.

Prescriptive performance environment: Playground.

Collective educational models: Teaching staff.

Multi-responsive environmental manager: Caretaker.

Quality assurance monitor: Picture of the Queen over the Principal's desk.

Individualised artistic expression: Graffiti.

Masticated mineral deposits: Chewing gum on class wall.

Environmental protector receptacles: Rubbish bins.

Visual analysis feedback studio: School library.

Spontaneous instructional indicator: School bell.

Quantitative density formula: Number of kids in class.

DOBBING

I have this information from our resident dobbing specialist. Dobbers are informers. Junior grass. They report to authority. This doesn't include Mother. Sorry about that!

It's playground politics and, like all things, some players go over the top and use dobbing as a threat for personal gain. Example: 'Sally, give me your chips or I'll dob to Miss Spencer you talked in class.' Chipless Sally needs to role-play with mummy, because she thinks the naughty thing was talking in class. Teach her to respond, 'No, I'm going to tell my mother you threatened me.' Vary the threat until she gets it right.

Talking of dobbing, I would like to thank Mrs Glass of Terranora Road for telling the ballet teacher that I *can* sew ...

BULLYING

You will not be told by your child if this is happening. Signs are varied.

- Not wanting to go to school.
- Nightmares.
- Wet knickers/skid marks in pants.
- Unusual behaviour.

Usually the first person to tell you is your child's friend's mother. Act immediately. Go to the teacher with your suspicions. Most schools have a policy on bullying. Unfortunately there are horrid children, usually the offspring of horrid parents, and neither the school nor you can change this. So it will invariably be *your* child who sees the School Counsellor and *your* child who changes classrooms. It's unfair, but heck, if it solves the problem, who cares?

BOOK CLUB

I will not be subjected to this subversive form of marketing. I don't care if the school gets a rake-off. I don't care if Mandy Simpson is getting the $15.95 pony book with the silver charm and the horse stickers.

What to Do

Don't say 'no' straight off. It's the end of the day and children have been 'choosing' books from the delightfully artistic tempting brochure all day. Resort to bribery. Philosophical discussion versus the 'I wants' is a waste of time. I offered a visit to the library to borrow six books plus a special treat dinner of Big Mac and chips and ice-cream in exchange for refusing one book from book club. Then we cut out pretty pictures from the brochure and stuck them on paper—nicely disposing of temptation.

HOME TO PLAY

Only one thing to say. Give and take. Actually, that's two things. Having friends home to play after school is practically the best part of the day for children, but if it gets one-sided and everyone's at your house, drop a few hints. Big ones.

AFTER-SCHOOL ACTIVITIES

Monday's piano, Tuesday's gymnastics, Wednesday's ballet, Thursday's violin, Friday's netball, Saturday's soccer, Sunday's swimming—keep them busy—mum's a taxi driver—no time for reading—dinner's a rush . . . Good grief! You're all mad.

School is enough, at least until Year 3. Captain Grubbyhands, in his black plastic Mickey Mouse ears and an old curtain, should be in the garden with his trusty steed Rover, fighting the dreaded brumby catchers . . .

TUTORS

I know, it's tough admitting you can't do calculus. I thought they were renal stones. The school may give you a list of teachers who tutor—sometimes you can share one to reduce costs.

SAFETY HOUSE

The school will have a list of locations if this great service operates in your area. Safety Houses are subject to a police check before listing. They have a yellow sticker out front and inmates are home the hours children travel to and from school. They are, quite literally, a safe house for your child to go to for help. Make sure the child knows the sign and locations between school and home. If Safety House is not established near you, choose a home or shop on the child's school route where they can go if they are frightened.

SCHOOL COMMITTEES

This is where everybody in the room knows all there is to know about everything, the person in charge is named after a piece of furniture and the secretary taking minutes falls apart each time passing a motion is mentioned. I work with a committee of one. Me.

BEFORE AND AFTER SCHOOL CARE

This is a service offered to parents who work. Children are taken to school from the care centre and picked up at bell time. There's often ten or so children from the same school. The local council and school have details.

ROUND TABLES

This is when Principal Arthur and the Knights of the Long Faces call you in with young Lancelot to discuss the latter's progress and behaviour—which has been bad. Round Table is not a good invitation!

Phew. I'm schooled out. Plum tuckered. Think I'll crack a few ice-cubes with the Gordon's. A spot of tonic. A slice of lemon. It's very good for malaria, dontcha know? And I didn't learn that at school . . .

CHAPTER TWELVE

STORYTIME—A DAY TRIP
WITH SCHOOL

On Monday a note materialised requesting six dollars and a signature for the school excursion to Currumbin Sanctuary. On Tuesday Mrs Barton asked if I would be a helpful parent and accompany the class. Stupid half-asleep me thought she'd said, 'Would you like to borrow the computer during the holidays?' Quick as a flash, I was standing by the school gates in sensible shoes clutching a packed lunch. Me, Mrs Barton, Mr Arbuthnot and 63 seven-year-olds.

'What's your name?' I sneered at one.

'Nicholas.'

'Nicholas who?'

'Nicholas girls shouldn't climb trees,' he quipped and 63 kids dissolved into giggles.

The bus arrived. The driver was smiling but we soon fixed that.

'Yoohoo, Mrs Groff,' called Mrs Barton. 'Get on and make the children fill up from the back.'

I did as I was told. I'd heard about Mrs Barton. Sixty-three children ignored my pointing finger and sat exactly where they wanted.

'I'm not sitting next to Joel,', screeched Rebecca.

'Be quiet, Joel,' roared Mrs Barton.

'Sit down!' shouted Mr Arbuthnot. I sat down.

'I've forgotten my lunch,' wailed Amanda. I gave her a toffee.

On arrival Rebecca fell off the bus and sprained her ankle. We were presented with a wheelchair. Sixteen children fell over and demanded wheelchairs. Everyone else went to the toilet. I did a headcount. Nicholas was missing. Mr Arbuthnot found him in the gift shop buying a plastic zebra.

'I want to go on the train,' shouted Amy.

'Gregory's looking at me,' cried Rebecca.

'Be quiet, Joel,' yelled Mrs Barton.

'I've forgotten my lunch,' sniffed Amanda. I gave her another toffee.

We terrorised a sugar glider, a tawny frogmouth and a diamond python. Eric the keeper, who was wishing he had a cobra, asked searching questions.

'Why do you think snakes have a forked tongue?'

Hands shot up. Eric chose Nicholas.

'So the snake can pick its nose both sides at the same time, Sir.'

I was beginning to like Nicholas. I gave him a toffee.

'I want to go on the train,' whined Amy.

'Sit down!' yelled Mr Arbuthnot.

'Be quiet, Joel,' cooed Mrs Barton.

Then Amanda vomited.

'Yuk, poo, aah!' went the others. Amy raced around shouting 'Amanda's puked,' for the benefit of interested spectators.

'Come along,' chirped an oblivious Mrs Barton. 'Let's go in "Creatures of the Night".'

We did. Within seconds every child had disappeared. But we could hear them. Boy, could we hear them! A keeper strode angrily past.

'Have you seen their teachers?' he growled. We shook our heads, then hid outside and waited for him to chase them out.

'Lunchtime,' sang Mrs Barton.

'I want to go on the train!' shouted Amy.

'Gregory's taken my chips,' screeched Joel.

'Be quiet, Joel,' said Mrs Barton.

'Where's Nicholas?' said Rebecca.

Off went Mr Arbuthnot again.

I gave extra sandwiches I'd made to Amanda and Gregory, who'd given his lunch to a passing ibis. Mr Arbuthnot reappeared with Nicholas. He'd been showing his zebra to the wombat. Mr Arbuthnot downed three Aspirin from the first-aid kit and Mrs Barton took a slug from her thermos and hiccoughed loudly. Everyone went to the toilet again. Amanda threw up the sandwich and Rebecca fell out of the wheelchair.

'Train next,' sang an increasingly flushed Mrs B.

Drink bottles and lunch wrappers became airborne. To the great delight of the children Mrs Barton had sat in peacock poo and there was much sniggering as she strode ahead of us. The Pooed Piper!

'There will be no pushing or shouting,' ordered Mr Arbuthnot.

I don't think the Aspirin were working.

In a trice 63 children pushed and shouted their way on board, the train tooted loudly and we departed like a wild itchy centipede with limbs flailing through doors, hands snatching leaves from trees and enough hooting and hollerin' to wake the dead. Above it all I distinctly heard Mrs Barton bellowing, 'Be quiet, Joel!'

I held on tight and prayed the driver was on Prozac.

'You'd make a good teacher,' Mr Arbuthnot told me on the way home.

I smiled. How could I tell him that if I worked in a school, the busiest person would be the executioner.

CHAPTER THIRTEEN
HOLIDAYS

Yoo Hoo! Calling entreprunes ... We want a Mother's Holiday Retreat. A place with our own room, bathroom, TV, video and gorgeous meals at set times so we never have to make *any* decisions.

We'd like a heated pool, pleasant walks, beautician, masseur, hairdresser, gourmet tea and coffee, room service, the best wines, a video collection to choose from and a bowl of imported chocolates in every room. None of that fresh fruit nonsense please. Rules as follows: No visitors, no pizzas, no telephones and no postcards. Sounds divine!

SCHOOL HOLIDAYS
'We're all going on a summer holiday,
No more worries for a week or two ...'

Blow it out your ear, Cliff ...

It must be extremely unpleasant to hear one's mother express dread at the prospect of having you home for the holidays. So stop it! Maybe 'holiday' is the wrong word. You wouldn't actually call a trashed house, massive expenditure and a laundry explosion a holiday. Would you?

Guess what? I love the holidays! I adore visitors, children larking around and crazy unplanned days. I don't care about the house or if everyone wears dirty shorts three days running. Just think. No packed lunches, no uniforms to iron, no frantic mornings, no feeding troops at different times, and no homework.

Flopsy Bunny hates holidays. He gets extra attention. Baths. A new hair-do. Training sessions over jumps. Last year, after my husband read *The Horse Whisperer*, poor Flopsy was whispered into a swim program. To give Flopsy his due he swam two lengths and learned to float on his side, but he wasn't impressed with the swimming trunks or the snorkel.

Contingency Planning is the key to enjoying the holidays at home. This means plans have a chance of possible occurrence. They are not set in concrete, but if they happen, you are prepared, and you are not at the mercy of weather, sickness, football games, other people, blocked drains or a broken head gasket.

Before the Holidays

- Have hair cut so you won't look a fright in the window seat at Pizza Hut.
- Find out who will be around for play and sleepovers.
- Hire weekly videos—the best ones go in the holidays.
- Phone tourist attractions, skating rinks, whatever you *might* do, and ask costs, hours, hire fees etc. Write them down.
- Ensure you have one outfit washed and ironed in case of impromptu meal invitations—or you get to test drive a Porsche.
- Get tyres pumped up on car. Do this because men ask if you've done it. You know, if they are in charge of the wheel.
- Fill pantry. Slacken the budget a bit and buy goodies ready made.
- Ensure you have the 'doings' for a 'surprise' family of five coming to dinner. You'll need to have dry ingredients in the cupboard and meat in the freezer. A member of staff can safely be sent out for salad and fresh bread. One lives in hope.

Next make a list of things to do. I love lists, I have lists of lists. Of course, you may not do any of these things, but it is handy to be prepared when your brain is fried and someone asks, 'What can we do today?'

Never say 'Would you like to go to the beach?' One will shout 'Whoopee!' and two will turn noses up. Announce firmly 'We are going to the beach in one hour' and follow this by asking them to hang washing out. They will promptly disappear, without argument. Don't ruin your day by expecting teenagers to look as if they are enjoying themselves. Let them sit ten metres from you at the beach. Sulking breeds character.

Now we come to the fun part. I bet you've never done this. Plan the first week back at school. For yourself. Five days of mummy fun. Lunch with a friend. A grown-up movie. I allow at least one day for shopping. I try on the most expensive clothes, things I'd never wear and couldn't possibly afford. I tell the sales assistant whopping lies, and ask questions about in-house alterations. Then I say, 'No, it's not what I'm looking for, but thank you for your time.' It's so simple to entertain a mother after the holidays.

THE RAIN OF TERROR
Things To Do with Young Children on Wet Days

I grew up in England where it rained twice in 19 years—once for ten years and once for nine. My mother, the innovative procedure specialist, never noticed rain. She'd open the back door, ask us to clean our rooms and smile as we high-tailed it into the deluge. Perhaps she thought it would make us grow. Like daisies.

We called areas of garden after names on the shipping forecast— Ross and Cromerty were garages, Dogger the old apple tree, and German Bight the air-raid shelter. I was Grace Darling and rescued shipwrecked sailors, and my brother, Captain Johnson, piloted the stricken SS *Warwickshire* through the rockery. God. Just thinking of it makes me want to phone my brother and say, 'Wanna go out in the rain?'

My mother even put up tents in hailstorms. We had a waterproof groundsheet, transistor radio, 'gadgets' made from garden flotsam, hot meals delivered to the door and a very wet dog. One summer we spent eight weeks at the South Pole and fished for crabapples through the flaps. We got terrible stomach-aches. Gosh, I almost forgot the list.

I'm not big on taking children to movies, ice-rinks or indoor swimming pools when it's raining, because everyone else is there. And, do remember, littlies love to do the same thing again and again, so if an idea is running hot, flog it to death.

The List

- Put up a waterproof tent, preferably before rain. Fill with plastic utensils, bowls etc. and give a picnic treat.
- Invite child's friends over on firm understanding they reciprocate tomorrow.
- Drape sheets and blankets over table to make a cubby. This can be a bolthole for the youngest evicted from outside tent.

- Have a disco. Pull curtains, dim lights and blast the woofers and tweeters.
- Make muffins. Children can do all of this except the oven part. They can be eaten in the tent—takeaway muffins.
- Throw an impromptu party. You'll be popular and well in credit in IOUs. Cook sausages and serve in hot dog rolls with sauce and a glass of coke. Buy a cake and cover it with candles. Don't organise games—it's not that sort of party.
- Make playdough (recipe later).
- Painting. No. Not the coloured stuff. Leave that for fine days in the garden. This involves a bucket of water, a proper brush and the inside of the garage wall. It's great on Besser brick.
- Make popcorn and watch a couple of videos. Pull curtains and turn sound up a bit to make like a regular cinema.

I could list a hundred innovative crafty ideas but, with young children, these are labour-intensive for mother. And boring. Much better to set the scene and let them create the dream.

How To Make Playdough
Half cup of plain flour.
Quarter cup of salt.
Two teaspoons of cream of tartar.
Two teaspoons of cooking oil.
Mix all together. Add a third of a cup of boiling coloured water (use egg dyes). Knead until smooth.

GOING AWAY
'I'm off now then, Marion,' my father used to say as he sailed out of Southampton Waters for the Southern Seas. Yes sirree. Pop never had to ask neighbours to put the bin out.

Men think when you go away you shut the door as you leave. And don't check to make sure it's locked. They try to program the video for a ball game on Tuesday, after you've unplugged all electrical equipment in case of lightning. Then they look at you 60 kilometres km down the road and ask, 'Did you bring my glasses?' You swallow hard, look out the side window and mumble '... and that's why I killed him, Your Worship.'

Checklist

- Return library books/videos.
- Ask neighbour to collect mail, water plants and put rubbish out. Give them a key and contact phone number.
- Stop milk and papers.
- Buy bottle of wine or chocolates to give neighbours when you get back.
- Organise pets—I farm out small fry to teenagers and pay a dollar a day. Praying for bereavement doesn't work. I've tried.
- Organise a cleaner to come in while you're away—the key is with the neighbour.
- Arrange for the lawn to be mowed. Give money to neighbour.
- Remove nasties from fridge.
- Unplug everything ...

PACKING

The English are not good packers. Years of denial and rectitude have taught us that if you get to Paris without an umbrella, then you get wet. It would never enter our heads to take one. Or buy one. This is why I was so impressed when I met my husband's family. Americans. Boy, did they know how to pack. No doing without there. They weren't even going to risk changing coffee brands. So in it all went—sheets, food, fishing tackle, spare lightbulbs, kettles, BBQs, spades. It was endless. You know those huge caravans you see Americans pulling on highways? Well, they're not caravans. It's just luggage.

I remember pointing out we'd probably be able to buy potatoes in Atlantic City. My father-in-law looked at me in shock and said, 'But we always buy our potatoes from Rutz market.' I felt a real underachiever with my Qantas cabin bag.

Mothers always take charge of packing. Otherwise it doesn't get done properly. You have to do it, for peace of mind.

Tips
- Pack men's things separately, otherwise they'll wreck *your* ironed clothes when they pull everything out.
- Make a list and stick to it. If you need something when you get there, buy it. Take list with you to tick off as you re-pack for home. Don't forget to list toys.
- If renting a holiday apartment, pack dishcloth and dishwasher powder. They never have any.
- Pack things the others will need on top—like swimmers. Then you can get rid of people while you unpack.
- Put everything into cases, even tennis racquets. Loose items are a pain.
- Label suitcases on the inside and outside. I've got cases that have travelled further on airlines than me, and I got one back from Nova Scotia only because I'd labelled the inside. Of course, *I've* never been to Nova Scotia.

A SHORT MACHINERY STORY
I have to tell you now, while it's fresh in my mind.

This morning I was told to check out mower prices, so I've just been tyre-kicking at the lawnmower shop. Old Victa 2-stroke has emphysema, probably because I left him outside in the rain.

Spotty Wayne, aged 17, was my salesman today. Wayne showed me the new Victa. He demonstrated the easy-start controls, the high-tech compressor, the 19-inch blade circle, the ball-bearing wheels and the stainless steel casing. And we mustn't forget the three-year warranty.

'Does it cut grass?' I asked.

Wayne didn't know.

'Would you like to lift it?' he said. 'It's very light.'

'Not really,' I said. 'I don't lift anything over three kilos unless it's crying.'

Salesman Wayne was a tad confused. They hadn't covered this conversation in his TAFE lawnmower course.

'Look, Wayne,' I said, 'what I really need is a few brochures, you know, with some figures and stuff. Just to show I've been here.'

'Why,' he asked, 'would you need to show you've been here?'

'It's a long story,' I said. 'Probably as old as time . . .'

The Maggie G. Packing Bee

This is simple. It works for trips one week and over.

Rule 1   Always pack for seven days, even if going for two months.

Rule 2   Each person has two items of the following clothing:

2 shorts	2 shirts
2 T-shirts	2 skirts
2 swimmers	2 jumpers (or 1 cardigan, 1 track top)
2 dresses	2 hats (1 cap, 1 sunhat)
2 pairs shoes	2 long pants (1 jeans, 1 track)

Now pack for each person:
1 lightweight rainjacket
1 warm jacket
underwear/socks

Exemptions are babies. Make your own master list to cover glasses, cameras, sports equipment, books, etc. I'd give you mine, but it's got things like 'rabbit's beach towel' and 'glass beer mug' on it.

PLANNING AND BOOKING

I should patent this sequence:

1. Father decides he'd like two weeks in Italy.
2. Children turn noses up.
3. Mother spends three weeks getting information, the best flights, good accommodation and preparing passports, money etc.

4.   Mother overhears father on phone saying, 'We're off to Italy.
     I managed to get cheap flights ...'

It's very sensible to take family holidays during school time. It's
cheaper and less crowded. I don't understand why parents get 'thingy'
about children missing a week or two of school. Of course school will
let you. The education department will naturally disapprove. But
teachers won't. One less child sounds mighty fine to them.

Don't ask. Tell. A simple note saying 'Mark will be absent 3
November to 18 November for a family holiday' will suffice. And
don't you dare ask for school work. This is a holiday ...

- Check Sunday papers—travel section is full of special
  offers.
- Don't go straight to an agent. Phone airlines and ask for
  discount offers, then phone travel agent, tell them when you
  want to go, and where, and see if they can match or better
  the price.
- Don't rely on agents for visa/passport information. Phone the
  consulate yourself. Twice.
- If flying between major cities, contact airlines and ask about
  packages. You can often get a return flight, three nights at
  the Sheraton plus a rental car for less than regular flight cost.
  You don't have to take the Sheraton or the car and you can
  often extend the return flight date.
- If booking a serviced holiday apartment, phone the resident
  manager and ask prices. Then phone back next day and make
  an offer—$50 less for the week. This only works in non-peak
  season.
- It is often cheaper, if you have four people, to take a taxi to
  the airport rather than public transport. Easier too.

STAYING IN SOMEONE ELSE'S HOME

As I've already said, this is not advisable if the someone else isn't
there. It's too stressful for mother. When staying with friends there
are two considerations:

- How wild are your offspring?
- How fussy are the hosts?

If the answer to either is 'very', reconsider plans. No sense in destroying friendships and spending a week with white knuckles.
   If you do stay, observe the following rules:
- Limit shower times.
- Hang wet towels outside.
- Purchase groceries—lots!
- Offer to cook.
- Make children clear away after meals—offer to wash up.
- Purchase a thank you gift.

And don't stay too long. Remember, houseguests are like fish—after three days they go off.

Thank You Gifts for Hosts
Check to see if they have one first ...

Suggestions

Earthenware water purifier	Good torch
Toasted sandwich maker	Electric carving knife
Four good beach towels	Beach umbrella
A board game	Good glass salad bowl
Picnic rug (rubber-backed)	Radio for bathroom
Picnic basket	A dozen bottles of great pickles
Rosebush (well established)	

You should spend at least $50 on whatever you get and always buy the best. It may seem an odd list but none involves the personal taste problem. And they're all useful.

CAR TRAVEL
Why are parents so pathetic about long car trips with children? So what if the progeny are bored, naughty, sick or fighting. Heavens,

I've been vomited on the entire way across North America, screamed at all the way to Melbourne and played 'I Spy' in every county in Southern England. Children are not the problem. It's getting Jackie Stewart to stop the car so you can go to the toilet—that's the problem.

You have three options:

1. Drive yourself.
2. Get catheterised.
3. Invent a urinary infection—one where you can't hold on . . .

And who packed the car? Mother's put everything in the boot. Father's put everything on the passenger side floor. You know why man landed on the moon, don't you? They were on their way to Mars but wouldn't ask directions . . . Need I say more?

Tips
- Ensure children can see from windows.
- Take singalong tapes.
- A bag of Minties in the glove box—no one can cry and chew at the same time.
- Bottled water only—you don't want sticky spills.
- Bribery. Promise a treat on arrival and follow through.

Car Games
'I spy with my little eye something beginning with P.'
  Answer: 'GRASS.'
  'It's my turn.'
  'You've just had a turn.'
  'No, I haven't.'
  THUMP
  'Mum!'
  'SHUT UP!'
The best game is where you don't have to say anything. It's called Three Things. Each child, in turn, picks three things to spot—for example, a cow, a bridge and a red car. Once they're spotted, the next

child chooses three new things. It's a clever game because there are no winners, and children don't notice you aren't playing.

AIRLINE TRAVEL

It is absolutely dreadful to be on a plane when a one-year-old is performing *King Lear* in row G. Once, on a flight between Bombay and London, there was a child going berserk, and nothing would placate her. The absolutely dreadful part was she belonged to me. Her father had thoughtfully placed himself in row B. I had, you see, taken advice and sedated her. No one told me this sedation game can have the opposite effect ... so be warned. At 15 months my daughter travelled to America without a peep, and then three months later went ape on a flight from Brisbane to Tamworth. You just never know.

Sedation

Yes, I continued to use sedation, but not for the flight. No point in the child sleeping all the way to London and being ready for action just as you keel over with exhaustion. Save sedation for arrival, so you can have a rest. Your doctor will advise what to give, but be careful— some countries are touchy about medications in luggage. I have a friend who was detained in Singapore for carrying a bunch of dried Australian flowers. One flower was a dried poppy. And you know what comes from poppies.

Tips

• Check what services airline offers for babies and children. Many supply nappies and colouring-in packs. If you require regular cow's milk you must notify them in advance. Pack disposable nappies anyway—I never trust airlines.

• If your baby requires made-up feeds and they aren't on solids yet, don't rely on the airline for supply—whatever they have told you. You'll need to pack a kit to last the whole journey. And then some. You don't want to be using foreign boiled water if the plane is delayed in Calcutta.

Buy at least a dozen baby bottles, sterilise, and fill with

boiled water. Invert sterile teat and cap. Place them upright in a plastic container (for emergency steriliser use) and put the lot in a chiller bag. Keep this with you at all times. Don't use the plane's fridge—your booty may be lost or shared. Place one large bottle of cooled boiled water in hand luggage as a back-up. Now you can make up each feed on the plane.

- Some planes have cots for babies under a certain weight. They pull out from the wall in front of you. Request these seats when booking.

- Case plane before take-off. You're looking for three empty seats together—perfect for a child to lie down and sleep. The stewardess will give you a pillow and blanket. Strap child in using middle seat belts. You will need five seats together for an adult snooze.

- Arm yourself with toys, puzzles etc. This sounds stupid but babies will sit on the floor and play for hours with an old handbag (one of those things you don't use any more), filled with bunches of keys, cards, hankies and the like.

- Take a change of clothes for yourself too—you don't want your arrival impression to be Eau de Babysick.

MOTION SICKNESS
I have a degree in motion sickness. My family chucked for Australia at the '86 Olympics.

Causes
Basically any erratic or rhythmic movement which creates a disparity between what the eye sees and the balance mechanism of the inner ear—moving horizons, reading in a car or staring sideways at fast passing landscape. Excitement, poor ventilation and fatty foods make it worse.

Symptoms
Nausea, headache, dizziness and vomiting.

Prevention

Motion sickness tablets, such as Kwells, are effective if taken an hour before travel. Another option is the Sea Band. You place one on each wrist—they exert controlled pressure on acupressure points. There are no side effects and they work in five minutes. Both tablets and bands are available from chemists.

Troubleshooting

I carry empty ice-cream containers with lids, so we can throw nasties into a passing town's rubbish bin. Have a wet face-cloth in a plastic bag, and spare plastic bags for dirty clothes. A severe case of motion sickness can be treated by lying the offender face down on solid ground—when you arrive at the destination.

THE PERFECT PICNIC

No, you are not going to spend three hours preparing food that will be dropped in sand or eaten in ten minutes. Mothers shouldn't do this any more. Pack butter, salad dressing, salad bowl, paper plates, cups, cutlery, breadboard, carving knife and booze requirements in the Esky or chiller bag. And the corkscrew. There. That didn't take long, did it? What? Food! Oh, you get that on the way . . .

- Cooked chicken.
- French loaf.
- Watermelon.
- Lemonade.
- Salad: cherry tomatoes, avocado, lettuce (preferably mesclun—this is different leaves, sold by the kilo)
- Tub of Kalamata olives (from deli section of supermarket)
- Corn chips

I told you it was the perfect picnic.

THE WEEKENDER

You've arrived. The house is paid off, the four-wheel drive is quivering in the garage and it seems the right time to invest in a holiday cottage. Fuzzy fantasies of beaches and fields, fresh air, time with the family, relaxing. Wait a minute—who's relaxing? It certainly isn't you.

Mother is doing the same things she does at home, only in a different place without proper equipment. Weekenders don't come with staff. There are now two homes to clean and two gardens to tend. Packing and unpacking. Food preparation. And don't forget the return to base, when everyone else settles down, wonderfully relaxed after a two-day sojourn, and mother prepares dinner, irons school uniforms and commences round one of the laundry . . .

No No No No No

No No No No

No No No

No No

No

CHAPTER FOURTEEN

SEALED SECTION

SANTA CLAUS

For years a fat old man with a white beard, rosy pink cheeks and red suit has taken credit for the wonderful presents delivered to our house on Christmas morning. This festive injustice has got to stop. Something, in fact, for the next Mothers' Union meeting.

Where was Fatso, I'd like to know, when I was lined up at K-Mart for 22 hours with a full bladder, shunting a trolley laden with toys, stocking fillers, wrapping paper and 'just-in-cases'. Ha! This year will be different. This year I want 'thank you'. I want intense gratitude. I want benediction.

Each year, as the jacaranda peppers a lavender carpet on the lawn, we prepare a letter to Santa. Priceless childish notes that I cherish and hide in my grandmother's jewel box. It seems I've hidden the last. This year's offering is a computerised readout headed, 'Submission for Santa '99'. Some items have a price and a catalogue page number.

The Cabcharge Chick, aged nine, although equipped to surf the net and on first name terms with the bank manager, is still a firm believer. I know this because we talked about it.

'Mum, you know Santa?'

'Not in the Biblical sense, darling.'

'Well, it's really Daddy, isn't it?'

'Of course not. Children who don't believe won't get any presents.'

'Okay.'

Hasn't she ever wondered why Santa and I use the same wrapping paper? Isn't it odd the Europeans next door get a special delivery on Christmas Eve? Hasn't she figured out where I hide the booty? For heaven's sake, we don't even have a chimney.

I think it's a snow job. Do you think it's a snow job? Nah! I take responsibility for perpetuating the myth. On Christmas morning I stomp around clearing up dead leaves and branches from the floor, mumbling distasteful remarks about reindeer and disrespect for carpet. Sometimes I've seen Santa in the night sky. Daddy has spoken to him. Twice. One year there was a torn piece of red fabric snagged on the door frame. Virtual reality. Perception is everything.

This year will be different. I will take glory for the big stuff, the bicycle or the new puppy, while Santa can be praised for Connector Pens. I've absolutely had it with Hirsute Ho Ho getting all the credit. Just one problem. How am I going to explain that Santa brought me an antique 18 carat rose gold bracelet with an emerald-studded clasp when Daddy only got me an electric sandwich griller?

Santa's Australian Address
Santa Claus

North Pole

Send the letter off in late November and your child will receive a card from Santa before Christmas. It's Australia Post magic.

THE TOOTH FAIRY
The morning will surely arrive when you awake to the woeful cry, 'Mummy, the Tooth Fairy didn't come.'

Whoops!

There follows frenzied groping under the child's pillow while you quickly deposit a coin that, not five seconds earlier, was tucked coldly in your purse. You mumble reproofs, 'Silly Tooth Fairy made it very hard to find,' and 'She always leaves the fourth tooth behind for you to keep.' You finally exclaim, 'Look! Here it is!'

You are awash with guilt for this dastardly crime against motherhood. You don't tell anyone, unless of course you're me, but then I'd have put my hand up to Watergate if I thought there was a free trip to Disneyland in it.

Make a sign saying:

REMEMBER
THE
TOOTH
FAIRY!

I have developed a scientifically proven system called Tooth Fairy Insurance. Take it out. Now.

1. Place a coin in a drawer beside your bed.
2. Place a coin in a mug on top shelf of kitchen cupboard.
3. Make the sign 'Remember the Tooth Fairy' and tack it to inside of kitchen cupboard where the mug is.

When the sprogling's tooth falls out, go straight to the cupboard, retrieve the sign and put it on the bathroom mirror where you clean your teeth at night. Interrogation can be placated with, 'It's to remind me to leave the window open for the tooth fairy.' You have the coin ready in the mug.

In the event you are sick/drunk/upset or too tired to clean your teeth, you still have the coin in the drawer to grab in the morning.

Smart, eh?

EASTER BUNNY

We are lucky. The Easter Bunny hides only the best-quality chocolate eggs in our garden. I expect he's learned from experience that cheap chocolate contains nasties that send little children crazy.

I love it how he leaves footprints on the driveway. It's just as if a grown-up has sprinkled flour everywhere and then made paw prints by pressing the tips of the middle three fingers together, centre one on top, and dotted them hoppingly in the flour. Yep. That's what it looks like.

CHAPTER FIFTEEN
FOOD

I like a drink when I'm cooking,
One or two at the most,
Three I'm under the table,
Four I'm under the host!

Before starting, I have to tell you about Lucy. A food tale, of sorts. Lucy is one of life's gorgeous creatures. A figure to die for, brown doe eyes, porcelain skin and black wavy hair you could surf. And a cracking cook to boot. So her husband left her. For the sexatary.

Local hounds came baying, and before you could say 'woof woof' Lucy had her first date in 20 years. She decided to meet on home turf and cook a meal.

Lucy renovated the house and herself. Fresh flowers, new hairdo, spiffy clothes and, for the first time, a manicure with fabulous false nails. She prepared prawns in chilli coconut sauce with sourdough bread, snapper with watercress salad and fresh date torte.

Fifteen minutes to go. Lucy opened champagne and poured a glass. The room was chilly. She lit a fire. And set alight the nails on her right hand.

In panic, she plunged the stinking, blackened-mangled mess into the champagne glass.

'Hello,' said a voice behind her. 'The door was open so I came in . . .'

HOW TO BE THE MOST DELICIOUS THING AT YOUR DINNER TABLE

This is extremely important. You are not challenging the sumptuous food. Oh dear me, no. You are competing against wine. Menfolk will be gorging on plovers' eggs in aspic and a glazed quince terrine, but they will be sniffing wine, talking wine and one-upping wine. Quite frankly I don't give a rat's arse if I'm drinking tipple from grapes grown in 1936 on the northside of a Swiss hill and trampled by barefoot French virgins. I hope they had tinea.

I usually take a sip and say, 'Yuk, you can shove this back in the horse.' Such class.

Now do you see how important it is to be the most delicious thing at your table? Do you? Good. Buy an apron. Get ready at least an hour before guests arrive, put on the apron to protect your clothes and, just as the doorbell rings, remove apron and spray exotic perfume in your hair, just above the ears. Muss it around a bit. Now, when men greet you with kissy cheek cheek they are getting a headful of Chateau Mama, and you have got in first.

MASTER SHOPPING LIST FOR MOTHERS

I prepared this 15 years ago when I worked a 40-hour week for the Department of Health. Now that I work 112 hours a week for Groff Inc it's even more useful. Why have I included it? Well, let's not forget I lived next door to Miranda, the professional air-head. Miranda never had the right ingredients. For anything. The list does not include fruit, vegetables or meat, but it will provide the basics for anything from lasagna to laksa.

Toilet rolls
Aluminium foil
Greaseproof paper
Paper serviettes
Paper plates

Bleach
Washing powder
Ajax
Dishwashing
  powder
Polish
Washing-up
  liquid
Insect repellent
Matches
Lightbulbs

Tinned
  Red kidney beans
  Sardines
  Tomatoes
  Corn
  Whole beetroot
  Baked beans
  Spaghetti
  Asparagus soup
  Sliced mango
  Apricot halves
  Coconut cream/
    milk
  Condensed milk
  Sauerkraut

Kebab sticks
Batteries

Cup-a-soup
Tomato puree
Lasagna noodles
Tagliatelle
Spirals
Elbows
Tubular spaghetti
Rice vermicelli
Family pack instant
  noodles
Rice
Hokkien noodles

Cardamom pods
Chilli powder
Ground cloves
Bay leaves
Dried lime leaves
Dried lemon grass
Oregano
Laos powder
Ground thyme
Tartaric acid
Citric acid
Custard powder
Saffron
Marjoram
Ceylon curry
  powder
Paprika
Turmeric
Green curry paste
Fennel seeds
Salt
Black pepper for
  grinder

Plain flour
Self-raising flour
White sugar
Caster sugar
Icing sugar
Brown sugar
Demerara sugar
Cooking chocolate
Red lentils
Popcorn

Vanilla essence
Rum essence
Black cumin seeds
Fenugreek
Ground coriander
Ground ginger
Ground cardamom
Allspice
Five spice powder
Mustard seeds
Cumin seeds
Cumin powder
Sesame seeds
Cinnamon
Nutmeg
Sage
Garam masala

Cordial
Lime juice
Apple juice
Cranberry juice
Tea
Coffee
Ovaltine

Soap
Shampoo
Conditioner
Toothpaste
Razors
Shaving cream
Bandaids
Dettol
Floss
Tampons
Aspirin

Almond meal
Sultanas
Jelly
Muffin mix
Dried yeast
Baking powder
Bicarbonate soda
Beef stock cubes
Chicken stock cubes

Vegemite
Golden syrup
Maple syrup
Nutella
Peanut butter
Honey
Marmalade
Jam for
   Skullduggery

Vanilla ice cream
Frozen peas
Frozen spinach
Frozen pastry
Apple pie
Fagottini

1 dozen eggs

Tabasco
Cranberry sauce
Black bean sauce
Mustard
Olive oil
Peanut oil
Balsamic vinegar
Salsa
Tomato sauce
Mayonnaise
Horseradish
Capers
Sesame oil
Soya sauce
Pickles
Grated ginger
Worcestershire
   sauce
Bottled artichokes
Holbrooks Oriental
   Stir Fry Sauce

Rum
Red wine
White wine
Marsala

Pretzels
Crackers
Biscuits
Muesli bars
Corn chips
Weet Bix (rabbit!)
Muesli
Sustain
Pine nuts
Walnuts

Orange juice (fresh)
Grated parmesan
Good vintage
   cheddar
Vanilla yoghurt
Cream
Milk
Ghee (clarified
   butter)
Kalamata olives

Tips
- Buy Asian spices from Asian shops. They are fresher.
- Keep herbs and spices in the dark. Third drawer down in the kitchen is a handy spot. Label the tops.

HERBS

There are two schools of thought in herb cookery. One puts fresh herbs in at the start of cooking and the other at the end. I'm an end girl. The taste is stronger, and fresh green adds a professional touch.

When we moved to the tropics I planted a herb garden in the rich volcanic soil. Flopsy Bunny was in heaven. One night I met Paralysis Python in the basil patch. Now I have big pots outside the back door, a torch, and a very large rake.

In this climate parsley, mint, oregano and rosemary grow forever. I re-seed basil every four months and coriander, a real ballerina, I replant the first of every month so I always have a plentiful supply. I don't plant pennyroyal because it causes abortion in cows, and as our garden is a haven for livestock I don't want to take unnecessary risks.

I very much need to speak to the person who has relabelled my latest batch of Skullduggery Jam 'Lemon Crud'.

A GIFT FOR LIFE

It is monstrous that hurried lives dictate frequent provision of tasteless, reckless offerings. Teaching your family the pleasure of preparing and eating good food is a grand endowment.

My favourite times are spent in the kitchen with my daughter. We pick and stew apples, cry buckets over horseradish and shuck peas across tables. 'Pop' they go, then 'plop plop plop' into the metal colander. Strawberries are husked, bowls are licked and tables are set. Two kitchen fairies. Wondrous stuff.

Once we picked and stewed pears with Grandma Groff in upstate New York. My mother-in-law's method was easier than mine. I have always found pears difficult to handle—slippery and prone to mush. Stella showed me, as with so many things, the correct way to do it.

My husband's family live in one of those pretty white houses Americans do so well. Attic windows rest cool in the shadow of sleepy elms, wooden chairs relax lonely on the porch and a lazy woodpile leans idle against the western wall counting its last days in the summer sun. Out back, knots of cherries and pears meander along squirrel paths to the old railroad track where once a day in late afternoon a solitary freight train rattles past, cheered on its way by happy hour of Bloody Marys made with homegrown tomatoes.

Behind geranium window boxes and dark green shutters beat the hearts of hunter-gatherers. For generations Groff women have preserved summer produce for lean winter months while men hunt deer and wild turkey to fill massive freezers that rumble hungry in the basement. And one must never be amused that it takes $4000 worth of camouflage outfits to capture one 'free' Thanksgiving turkey. There are some things you just don't laugh at in America.

One year our holiday coincided with pear picking, although my father-in-law mentioned sadly that for the last couple of years there hadn't been much fruit. Early one morning we dispatched men to golf and Stella announced we would 'do' pears. Off she went down the garden, granddaughter in one hand and a bushel basket in the other.

A $4000 AMERICAN TURKEY.

We picked pears. And we picked pears. And then we threw them over the railroad tracks.

'I've got better things to do than stew pears,' said Stella, and she took her precious granddaughter and they sat in the grass and played and ate wild strawberries while I hid the bushel baskets in the garage.

The men returned at five and we sat in the garden drinking cocktails. At five-thirty I heard the distant hum of a train. Stella and I smiled knowingly as it hurtled past, stewing our pale green harvest to smithereens.

'Ah,' said Stella, planting a kiss on her granddaughter, 'I think we'll do the pears tomorrow.'

WHERE TO HIDE FOOD

This is exactly the sort of thing that should be taught in schools as part of female sex education. Not the anatomically correct nonsense. What am I talking about?

Listen up. I'm talking about mother who, with organisational foresight, pre-prepared the evening meal and refrigerated it at 10 a.m. Then she went out. Meantime, starving Russia returns from a golf game with friends and they consume the lot for lunch . . .

Working on the principle that men and teenagers can't find socks in their sock drawer, it shouldn't be too hard to hide food in the fridge. Wrong! These people have restaurant-grade radar. Now, you have to promise never to show this page to my family. Okay.

For Your Pies Only

If I haven't used the oven, I pack cooked food in blue ice packs and put it in the cold oven. (When did anyone in the house but you open the oven door?) If the oven is hot I use an Esky in the back of the pantry. Four ice packs are enough for several hours. Place newspaper on top and two pairs of old shoes on the Esky for camouflage.

'I'M THE PRESIDENT OF THE USA AND I WON'T EAT BROCCOLI ANY MORE!'

Yes. This is the only excuse for refusing vegetables. I think it was said by President Bush. I hope so. He was my favourite. I apologise if it was another chap, but you have to say good things about women to get in my book. Who could forget George Bush's acceptance speech for the Republican Nomination when he told American women they were gaining equality through economic empowerment and he wouldn't let anyone take it away. That's my man.

I met him once you know, George Bush. Well, he drove past and I smiled. Close enough. It was in Kennebunkport, Maine, in 1991. He looked great, even without the broccoli. Can you believe there's a place called Kennebunkport?

Since time began, mothers have invented ways of forcing children to eat fresh vegetables. We send them to bed without food, punish in a squillion useless ways and rave about starving babies in Africa. Nothing works.

I have been moderately successful in this department, though my methods are unconventional and probably against the law. I used to scatter sliced carrot, celery, lettuce and cherry tomatoes on the floor. Sounds awful, but when you think an average baby will eat a bucket of sand a day at the beach, I didn't see any harm in turning the kitchen into a giant plate. Anyway, it worked.

As my daughter got older I resorted to bribery. You know, I'll give ice-cream if you eat green beans. I never threatened and never punished if she couldn't follow through. My reward is a nine-year-old who will try any food once, and has a genuine love of fine cuisine. Why, only the other day I said, 'I'll give you a dollar if you eat that chargrilled baby octopus.' She ate six. It's her Culinary Savings Plan.

Simulacrum Sponge

Look it up, you lazy devil.

Purchase an unfilled two-layer sponge from the supermarket.
Spread bottom layer with strawberry jam.
Whip thick cream (not lite) until it peaks firmly.
Spread this over jam.
Place top on gently.
Sift icing sugar over the top.

I made it myself ...

Hoax Hummus

I purchase hummus from the deli and transfer it to my own Pyrex dish when unpacking shopping. The mythology is so entrenched I have seen my husband tip it into the Pyrex dish without once considering I haven't made it. Maybe he thinks I do something brilliant to it later.

I have been told a certain well-known literary agent has been misleading family and friends for years with 'her' tabbouleh.

Oh gosh! Sorry Selwa—It just slipped out ...

FOOD ADDITIVES

I wish to extend a party invitation to scientists from the Sulphur Dioxide Company of Soda Springs USA, who recently published a research paper proclaiming food colourings do not affect small children.

Party Details

There will be ten children. I will provide red cordial and yellow snacks. Then I shall let the scientists take the children home ...

Meanwhile, in the real world, we at the University of the Bleeding Obvious know certain food additives create a downhill trajectory on the good-behaviour curve. (Sorry, but I'm having to use researchy type words here.)

What's What?

- Additives—added to food to improve quality, presentation, storage and flavour. Both natural and artificial additives can cause adverse reactions.
- Preservatives—used to control mould, yeast and bacteria growth. Salt, sugar and vinegar are natural preservatives. Sulphur dioxide (220), used in cordial, fruit juice and dried fruit may cause reactions.
- Antioxidants—used to prevent fat or oil becoming rancid when exposed to oxygen. Vitamin C (L-ascorbic acid 300) is a common antioxidant.
- Colours—most food colours are derived from natural substances. They are used to make food look appealing. However, Red Rager, Green Death and Yellow Berserker (my names) do incite children to riot. Tartrazine (102), a yellow colour, can also cause headaches, itching, asthma attacks and extreme wakefulness.
- Flavouring agents—produce odour and/or taste. Flavours are natural, nature-identical or artificial. Monosodium glutamate (621) is a flavour enhancer used in savoury foods, stock cubes and dried soups. It may cause thirst, nausea, headache, fainting and dizziness. Great, eh.
- Emulsifiers—prevent separation of oil and water in foods such as ice-cream, sauces and low-fat spreads.
- Stabilisers—used to thicken foods. Agar (406) is a natural stabiliser from seaweed.
- Sweeteners—there are five currently approved for use in Australia: saccharin, cyclamate, aspartame, acesulphame potassium and thaumatin. You really needed to know this, didn't you?

A list of additives and their numbers can be obtained from your State Department of Health.

MY SECRETS REVEALED

How to Make Maggie's Gravy

Place two unpeeled cloves of garlic in roasting pan at start of cooking. When meat is cooked, take it out to stand for about 20 minutes. Pour meat juices into a saucepan. Scrape innards out of garlic and discard skin. Add innards to meat juices. Place saucepan on low heat and stir in two tablespoons of flour. Continue stirring and slowly add a glass of wine (red or white). Season with freshly grated black pepper. Add herbs such as fresh rosemary or dried oregano. Add ¾ cup of water a little at a time, and continue stirring until you have required texture. (If I have boiled green vegetables I use this water instead.) Voila!

How to Make Maggie's Secret Salad Dressing

This should save you about $70 on the annual grocery bill. It is most important you keep to correct oil and vinegar proportions.

Six tablespoons of extra virgin olive oil.
Two tablespoons of balsamic vinegar.
Quarter teaspoon of salt.
Freshly grated black pepper.
Two peeled and sliced cloves of garlic.

Put all ingredients in a bottle and shake shake shake. Do not refrigerate. Shake well before use. If you don't like a dark-coloured dressing you can substitute white wine vinegar for the balsamic. But it's not as good.

Maggie's Krakatoa

This is a perfect breakfast I developed in my nursing days when I could no longer stand the sight of boiled egg or milk dribbling down comatosed chins.

Place half a cup of muesli in a bowl.
Pour half a cup of yoghurt over muesli.
Top with chopped fresh fruit.

Naturally, you will never have time to eat this.

Stop Press

I have just discovered perfect rice. Oh, blast. I went to get the packet so I could write it down for you and now I have rice all over my desk. Looks like an albino mouse passed this way. It's called Taj King Golden Rice Basmati Parboiled. And it really truly works. And you know what else? It tastes nice too.

Almost forgot. You do realise that rice does not need to be served hot—room temperature is fine. In fact it's preferable, especially with hot curry. Restaurants have been doing this for years. You just never noticed.

FRUIT AND VEGETABLES—BUYING AND STORAGE

Apples	Select firm fruit, free of bruises. Large apples do not keep as well as smaller fruit. Smell is a good indication of flavour. Store at room temperature or in vented plastic bag in fridge.
Apricots	Avoid soft, shrivelled or dull fruit. Skin should be bright apricot, firm and plump. They deteriorate quickly at room temperature, so store in fridge in an open bowl.
Avocados	Choose dull-skinned fruit that 'gives' on slight pressure. Very soft fruit will be black inside. Ripen at room temperature. In general, those with dark bobbly skin have the best flavour.
Bananas	Select bright, medium-sized, well-rounded fruit free of bruises. Store at room temperature. Skin blackens on refrigeration. Overripe bananas make the best cakes.
Beans	Choose firm, long straight pods that 'snap'. Store in plastic bag in fridge.
Blueberries	As a rule these are only available when in season, and then they are all delicious.
Bean Sprouts	These should be firm and fresh-looking. Store in plastic bag in fridge and use as soon as possible.

Broccoli	Pick compact flower heads with no yellow. Leaves and stem should look fresh. Keep dry and do not over-handle. Store in vented plastic bag in fridge.
Brussels Sprouts	Select firm, compact, bright green sprouts—those with a vague purple tinge are excellent. Store in plastic bag in fridge.
Cabbage	Pick firm solid heads with strong outer leaves. Trim off outer leaves and store in plastic bag in fridge.
Capsicum	Choose well-shaped, thick-walled, firm, glossy capsicum of uniform colour. Store in plastic bag in refrigerator. They do not store well once cut.
Carrots	Use the bendy test. Carrots should be very firm, smooth, medium-sized and deep orange. Store in plastic bag in fridge.
Cauliflower	Choose firm white compact heads with no spots or bruises. Remove leaves before storing in plastic bag in fridge.
Celery	Select crisp firm stems with fresh leaves. Wash, trim and store in plastic bag in fridge. Celery can also be stored in a bowl of ice water in the fridge.
Cherries	Choose bright uniform-coloured fruit with firm texture. Stems should be green. Store in vented plastic bag in fridge. Use as soon as possible.
Cucumber	Select green (with no yellow colouring), firm, fresh-looking cucumbers. Store in fridge.
Eggplant	Select dark purple to black skin colour with firm texture. Store in cool dry place or in crisper.
Grapefruit	Choose heavy firm fruit with bright yellow smooth skin. Give the 'sweet smell' test. Store in cool place or in crisper.
Grapes	Select uniform-shaped bunches of firm smooth grapes with green stems. Store in vented plastic bag in fridge. Use as soon as possible.

Kiwi Fruit	Select firm heavy fruit with no bruising. Store at room temperature.
Lemons	Choose firm, heavy, fine-textured fruit. Store in a cool dry place.
Lettuce	Select firm green heads with crisp outer leaves and a 'solid' heart. Store in plastic bag in fridge or wash and place in lettuce crisper.
Lychees	Select clean-looking dark red fruit that 'gives' slightly under pressure. Store in vented plastic bag in fridge.
Mandarins	Pick heavy firm fruit with glossy skin. The heavier, the juicier. Store at room temperature or in crisper.
Mushrooms	Choose firm white or creamy mushrooms. Keep dry. Store in paper bag or Pyrex container with lid in fridge.
Nectarines	Choose highly coloured fruit with no blemishes. Ripe fruit will 'give' under slight pressure. Nectarines bruise easily. Store at room temperature and use as soon as possible.
Onions	Choose onions with firm clear outer skin with no sign of sprouting. Store in cool, dark place.
Oranges	Select heavy firm fruit with glossy fine-textured skin. They should smell sweet. Store at room temperature or in crisper.
Passionfruit	Select heavy full fruit with smooth dark skin. Avoid withered skin. Store in plastic bag in fridge.
Pawpaw	Choose well-coloured skin free of bruising. Fruit should smell sweet. Ripen at room temperature.
Peaches	Select firm fruit which has a peachy aroma. Avoid bruises. Peach will 'give' under slight pressure when ripe. Store in crisper.
Pears	Apply gentle pressure at the stem. Slight 'give' indicates ripeness as pears ripen from the inside out. Ripen at room temperature and store in crisper.

Peas	Choose bright green pods with smooth skin. Store in plastic bag in fridge.
Pineapples	This fruit does not ripen after picking. It merely starts to rot. Select fruit that has a sweet aroma and is tender to pressure near the stem. Store in cool dry place or refrigerate.
Plums	Select firm uniform-coloured fruit with no wrinkles. Ripen at room temperature and use as soon as possible.
Potatoes	Green potatoes are poisonous. Skin should be firm, unbroken with no shoots. Store in a cool, dry, dark place, not the fridge.
Pumpkin	Choose firm bright flesh. Store in cool dry place until cut. Then remove seeds and place in plastic bag in fridge.
Radishes	Select bright-coloured bunches with fresh-looking leaves. Top and tail radishes and store in a bowl of cold water in fridge.
Rockmelon	Choose fruit with a sweet aroma and no soft spots. Ripen at room temperature and store cut melon in Pyrex dish in fridge.
Spinach	Choose glossy, dark green leaves with no limp parts. Stems should look 'fresh'. Remove stems, wash and store in plastic bag in fridge.
Strawberries	Choose firm brightly coloured fruit with no dark patches. Store in fridge. Use as soon as possible.
Sweet Corn	Avoid dried-up withered-looking cobs. Kernels should be full and juicy. Store in plastic bag in fridge and leave husk on until needed.
Tomatoes	Select heavy, firm fruit free of marks. Ripe tomatoes are a uniform deep red colour. Store at room temperature for increased flavour.
Watermelon	Select large, heavy, well-coloured fruit. Store in cool place and refrigerate once cut in a large bowl with a lid (I use a large salad bowl and saucepan lid).

| Zucchini | Choose firm well-shaped zucchini with glossy skin and solid colour. Store in plastic bag in fridge. |

AN EVENING OUT

There is nothing quite so torrid as preparing a meal for the children before you go out to dinner. It's bordering on smotherhood. Personally I never met a frozen pizza I didn't like but, even so, fisticuffs will ensue if you do not supervise.

The Solution

It's quite simple. The babysitter should arrive one hour before you leave. They feed the five thousand while you get ready.

You will be pleased to know I have put on six kilos while writing this chapter. If I read or write about food the fridge door gets a workout. When I was reading *A Year in Provence* by Peter Mayle I overdosed on cheese, red wine and olives and by page 94 I was taller when I was lying down. Practically a continent.

SERVIETTE FOLDING FOR THE TOTALLY EXHAUSTED

Every mother should know at least one fancy way of folding serviettes. It shows you 'once' went to a restaurant. Here are two easy and impressive methods.

Fleur-de-lis

1. Open serviette to lie flat. Fold in half diagonally with point towards you. Fold top corners down towards point.
2. Fold same two corners in half away from you so points meet at top.
3. Roll bottom layer over two or three times towards centre.
4. Bend ends towards back and secure with paperclip.
5. Turn down loose flaps and tuck into collar.

FLEUR DE LIS

1.

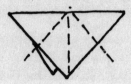 then

2.

3.

4.

5.

Sydney Opera House

1. Use serviette as folded in packet.
2. Place on table with four loose points towards you.
3. Fold in half away from you.
4. Fold in sides so long side edge meets triangle midline.
5. Fold under bottom points.

6. Fold back on middle crease and secure underside with paperclip.
7. Now pull up points individually.

SYDNEY OPERA HOUSE

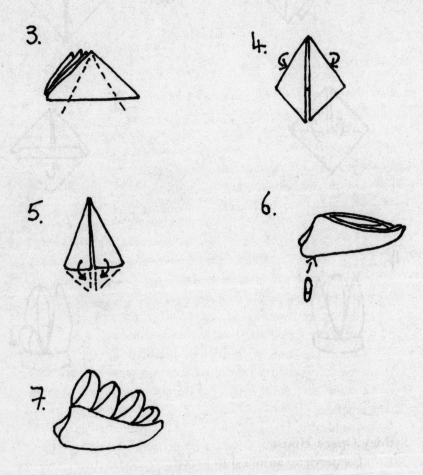

Yes, yes, I know. It's just too brilliant for words, isn't it.

DINNER AT 'OME

Even if you have avoided the maternal catastrophe created by excessive after-school activities, the notion of a family dinner at six is still a challenge. You will be thwarted by thwartables—visitors, playmates, extra mouths, adult commitments, P and C meetings, etc. etc. And we must not forget age disparity among diners and respective bedtimes.

The Problem

Yes, it's *indoctrination* again. The pressure to be Norman Rockwell mothers carving chicken at the head of a family table is alive and well in suburbia. Meat and two veg rules supreme in the house of Bruce and Kylie Sixpack.

The Solution

Teach yourself to provide good food on busy nights that can be prepared in one hit and 'staggered' to accommodate time schedules.

Examples

- Cook a joint of beef and slice it. Serve cold with pickles, salad, fresh damper and rockmelon and ice-cream to follow.
- Sliced ham off the bone from the butcher, two salads, wholemeal cob and strawberries and cream to follow.
- Homemade minestrone soup with parmesan cheese. Serve with fresh bread and banana cake for dessert.
- Curry, rice and salad. Rice is prepared ahead of time and served cold. Curry can be reheated on stove top as required. Follow this with fresh fruit in season—grapes, cherries or peaches.
- Spaghetti bolognaise. Old faithful. Spaghetti can be cooked at first sitting and reheated by pouring boiling water over it in the colander. Bolognaise sauce is reheated on stove top. Serve with parmesan cheese and salad with fresh fruit to follow.
- Prepare hamburgers and grill as required. Serve on fresh bakery rolls with salad. Follow with fruit and ice-cream.

- Prepare kebabs and grill as required. Serve with fresh bread, salad and follow with fruit in season.

Are you getting the hang of this now?

Tips
- Buy fresh bread from bakery. Carve at table as required—this looks more appetising than pre-sliced doorstops.
- Vary salads. Use your imagination and add tinned artichokes, sliced mango, pine nuts or snow peas. Sprinkle with fresh herbs that are now growing outside your back door.
- Jack, aged three, is eating on his own. Sit down and read to him as he eats and, boy, will you get payback when he learns to read at school.
- Sure as eggs someone won't like your menu. Tough.

Let them eat bread . . .

CHAPTER SIXTEEN

THE HOME FRONT

The time has come the Walrus said,
To talk of love and marriage.
And change the blasted family room,
Back to a double garage.

Loose Cannon—1998

I'm coming back as an architect. My husband is coming back as our panel beater. Suits me. He can hammer away while I straighten the Leaning Tower of Pisa with my Viagra Irrigation Plan. I wonder why architects wear bow ties. A security measure perhaps? To avoid strangulation.

As I write, acres of pale mud-magnet carpet are laid in family rooms adjacent to kitchens so no one can hear televisions above dishwashers.

A hundred metres distant is the marble bathroom where one drop of spilled water occasions head injury and laceration and, as if that wasn't enough, knobs have been placed at the base of stair banisters so you no longer slide off the end. They're known in the trade as Federation Injury Posts.

Only one thing for it. We must lock a mother of four in the architecture department at Sydney University and say, 'You can't come out until you've designed a sensible house.' Then we patent it and from proceeds develop a garage on wheels that rolls over a parked car so I no longer get into trouble for offside dings.

THE KITCHEN

There's been a terrible crime. Someone has stolen the heartbeat from our kitchens. Picture this. An old-fashioned scullery. A big table centre stage, oodles of chairs, a crackling fire, plates warming over the oven and hats and coats and wellies in the corner. The very thought makes you want to rush in and bake bread. Okay, okay. Rush in and eat bread. (Yes, I had servants in my picture too.)

But someone had to wreck it. Kitchen police felled walls and chromed us into the corner of a vast void known as the family room where TV rules soundwaves and frowns furiously at blenders and sizzling onions.

In fact, I think I'll go down to the Gold Coast Display Village right now and make a citizen's arrest. They can share a cell with the last person who said, 'Come and look at this,' while I was wrist deep in pizza dough.

The Sink

Excuse me for breathing, but if man can fly to the moon, why do mothers still stand at kitchen sinks? Who are those morons that put doors in the way of a jolly good sit on a stool? There is plenty of leg room. Go and look. A footrest would be nice, too.

Cupboards

Never have glass doors on kitchen cupboards. These are strictly for homes photographed in *House and Garden*.

The Floor

Terracotta! Ceramic tiles! Strike me pink, don't these people ever have it off in their kitchens? A kitchen floor should have 'give' and 'warmth' to alleviate maternal skeletal stress from all that sink standing. I use the saucer test. If the saucer breaks when dropped from a height of six inches, the floor is not user-friendly. And how nice it is to finally discover a use for saucers since I turfed the pot plants.

The Pantry

This is not a cupboard with deep shelves for cultivating bacteria in packets at the back. Kitchens should have a large walk-in pantry, at least 1½ by 1½ metres, with shelves tin deep on one side and plate deep on the others. The light should turn on and off as doors open and close, like the fridge.

You can fit eight adults in my pantry. Proof that ageing flower children still know how to move and shake at a dinner party. Once, after an evening of ribald entertainment, I found graffiti on the pantry wall—'I'm quite attractive, I've got a good job and most of my friends like me. How come I'm married to such a shit?' I left it there. No one's owned up yet.

The Secret Cupboard

Historians believe secret passages in seventeenth-century houses were hidey spots for fugitive priests. Oh no, John, no, John, no. They were secret cupboards for mothers. To hide Christmas presents. Every home should have one. So come on builders, put imagination into the carpentry department.

THE MRS BEDROOM

Far be it from me to be politically correct but the term 'master bedroom' conjures images of Captain Rochester pleasuring Milady with his boots on. And another thing. I'd like to spend five minutes alone with the sadist who dreamed up the 'en suite'.

Where is the mother who enjoys relaxing on her top-of-the-range Tontines, sipping Earl Grey to the farmyard accompaniment of Captain Rochester's morning ablutions not a hop, skip and a jump from the matrimonial bed?

CHILDREN'S BEDROOMS

Admiral Lord Horatio Nelson would have loved the little boxes made of ticky-tacky that pass for children's bedrooms today. We used to visit his flagship *Victory* at Portsmouth quite often. It never ceased to amaze me how small he was and how minuscule his furnishings were. A tiny bed, tiny jimjams, tiny chairs and tiny tables in a great big stateroom. He probably had agoraphobia.

It was always a sad visit. On the deck is a raised brass plaque marking the spot of his death at the Battle of Trafalgar. It is simple and poignant, 'Here fell Lord Nelson 1805'. My mother was deeply moved by this. Once, shaking her head in despair, she muttered, 'I'm not a bit surprised it happened. I nearly fell over it myself.'

I digress from the subject at hand. Children's rooms need the following:

- Room for an extra bed for sleepovers.
- Lots of cupboards.
- A sink! Yes. A place to clean teeth and wash babies' bottoms.
- A wall covered in cork for posters etc.
- A full-length mirror for ballet enthusiasts and violin virtuosos.
- Wooden or cork floors. (Anyone who has spent two days sponging vomit from carpet will know what I mean.) They are also essential for tap-dancing, racing motor cars and making clop-clop horse sounds.

THE BATHROOM

Let's assume the average family has two children who grow up and provide four grandchildren between them. That's six children. And $6 \times 9 = 54$ years of 'small person' bathroom use over three generations. Is it too much to ask, in a new home with three bathrooms, for one sink, one shower faucet and one lavatory to be lower? Apparently.

And why no mirrors in showers? I'm sure men don't want to drip water across the bathrooms as they trip to the sink for a shave. But then again . . .

Archimedes' Principle

Not many people know this. I swear it's true. One day Archimedes noticed his wife was smelly.

'Eureka,' he shouted. 'Go take a batha.'

So Mrs A. took a bath. The rest is history. Physics law.

'If a body is immersed in a liquid, the phone rings . . .'

The Southern Territory

In the animal kingdom males mark their territory by depositing noxious scent. The human male, during tender years, fills this need by peeing gaily on toilet seats and surrounding floors. Age improves lavatorial technique only marginally. Get used to it.

Bathroom Tips for Mothers Who Iron Tea Towels

- Hang bath toys in mesh bag over bath so water drains out.
- Bubble bath will keep the bath clean. This is because your children are not dirty in the first place.
- Get a life.

Bathroom Tips for Mothers Who Don't Iron Tea Towels

- Install black bath, black tiles and black grouting. It saves years of time on mould cultivation.
- Purchase a good-quality rubber-backed bath mat. The white embroidered bathmat you stole from the Waikiki Surfsider will not be recognised as such by males, who will be using your best towels on the floor instead.

- Use thin towels. They are more absorbent, wash more easily, dry more quickly and are cheaper. The 'thick towel' nonsense has gone on long enough . . .
- Face washers shaped like mitts are easier for children to use.
- Teach little girls to wipe their bottoms front to back after using the lavatory. This prevents bacteria from the anus being transferred to the urinary tract.
- A red dot on your toothbrush will remind you to take contraceptive pills.

MAGGIE GROFF'S FIX-IT-BOX

This is my pretend shed. I fix everything except cats and, of course, now I've met the local plumber I shall be discarding the washers. It contains:

Araldite	Screwdrivers
Superglue	Pliers
Scissors	Electrical masking tape
Stapler	Safety pins
Stickytape	Dressmaker's pins
Black laundry marker	Sewing needle and white thread
Blu-Tack	Wooden skewers
Whiteout	Lightbulb
Elastic bands	Drawing pins
Bulldog clips	Tape measure
Paperclips	Ruler
Pens/pencils	Compass (metal drawing sort)
Nail clippers	Ball of string
Rubber	Pack AA batteries
Puncture repair kit	Picture hangers
Paintbrush	Plastic lids for glue mixing
Polyfilla	Penknife
Hammer	Torch
Fuses	Assortment of nails/screws
Sheet of sandpaper	Tap washers
Extension cord	Adhesive labels (for jam!)

Tweezers
Bandaids

Two pegs (for securing glued
    items)
Small tin of plastic wood

HOME SAFETY

I was nearly killed in a fire at my London nurses' home in 1971. Oh
all right. I wasn't there at the time—it was a busy era with Henley
Regatta, the Hurlingham Ball and all that jazz. I spent the night with
friends and several bottles of Pimms No. 1 in the children's playhouse
on the front lawn of the Hurlingham Club overlooking the Thames.

At 8 a.m. we were thrown out and I went home on the tube in my
ballgown—a common sight in London in the early 70s. I had mastered
the art of staying out all night but hadn't quite fine-tuned the getting
home part.

Anyway, I returned to find my clothes and possessions burnt to
cinders. That was me, too—Cinders. A ballgown, black patent Bally
shoes, Marks and Sparks undies and a beaded clutch purse. Poor little
waif.

SONGS OF EXPERIENCE
Bathroom

* Lower hot water temperature on thermostat.
* Never leave a baby or small child alone in the bath.
* Run cold water through tap after running bath to prevent metal scalds.
* Place rubber mat in bath to prevent slippage.
* Put lid on nappy bucket or, better still, place bucket in laundry tub. Children have drowned in buckets.
* Remove electrical equipment (hairdryers etc.) from bathrooms and fit safety plugs in power points.
* Discard unused medications and place rest in locked cupboard.
* Don't leave other children to supervise babies' baths.
* Place razors and other sharp objects out of reach.

Kitchen

- Knives, glasses and sharps should be out of reach.
- Oven doors get very hot, so beware.
- Household chemicals (kitchen, bathroom, garden and laundry) should be kept out of reach in a locked cupboard. Dishwashing powder is caustic and extremely dangerous.
- Immobilise cupboards with string, tape or kiddie-locks.
- Learn to use rear hot plates and keep saucepan handles towards back.
- Secure kettle or jug leads so they don't drape over benches. A cup hook can be fitted behind the kettle and the lead threaded through it for safety.
- Don't leave cups of coffee or tea on low surfaces.

General

- Stairs should be fitted with a safety gate.
- Install smoke alarms—a cheap safety precaution.
- Lower door handles so children can escape in a fire (many homes built in 1930 have door handles near the top.)
- Safety plug unused electrical sockets.
- Remove all breakables.
- Cover sharp corners with padding or plastic covers available at hardware stores.
- Don't put baby bouncers on tables. They rock off the edge when you're not looking.
- Caution if microwaving baby's bottles. This is unnecessary, but if you must do it, be careful. The milk gets hotter than you think.
- Secure bookcases by bolting the top to the wall.
- Blu-Tack a cork to each end of the piano lid to avoid slammed fingers.
- Apartment living? Secure children's windows so they cannot fall out.
- Gardening equipment—shears, secateurs, chemicals—should be well out of reach.

- Guard all fires. Never leave a child alone in a room with a fire, even if it is guarded.
- Keep lighters and matches on top shelf of kitchen cupboard.
- Do not leave a baby in a pram unattended in the garden unless you have a safety net cover to protect them from being smothered by cats.

The Beach and Swimming Pools

- Surf is dangerous. Never allow children to run into the surf and dive, even though 20 idiots are doing it in front of you. There are more spinal injuries caused by this stupid macho activity than from motorcycle accidents (donor cycle accidents).
- Teach your children never to dive in any water unless they know how deep it is.
- Never assume another adult is watching out for your child at the beach or pool. It is your responsibility. I have seen two babies nearly drown at pool parties where adults 'thought' someone else was watching their children.
- Babies and children must wear life-jackets at all times when on boats. My daughter wore a full life-jacket, which strapped between her legs, from the age of three months. It saved her life on one occasion when she fell in the Hawkesbury River. She even slept in it when we night sailed (the life-jacket, not the river).

THE TIMES WE DON'T TALK ABOUT

There may come a time when you can't take one more dirty nappy, one more cry or one more sleepless night. It may be compounded by financial worries, grief or an unfaithful husband. You are frightened of hurting your child. Here's what to do.

1. Put the screaming child in their cot where they are safe.
2. Walk out of the house.

3. When you have calmed down, go back in and ring a friend or partner to come immediately, then walk out of the house again and wait for them.

This is the right thing to do. So don't feel guilty.

MARKING YOUR TERRITORY

Yes. Boys do it. Let's do it. Let's make our mark ... Create a poster-size picture of yourself and the children. Be sure you look glamorous. Hang it in your husband's workplace, right where his female workmates can see it.

HOT TIP FOR A SEAMSTRESS

Trying to sew with toddlers around? Buy a playpen. A large one. Set the machine up inside the playpen. Yes, it's for you, not them.

MOVING HOUSE

I'm married to a man who knows a thousand ways to move house without using a furniture removalist van. I've carried three-seater sofas along Military Road, Mosman, hoisted beds over balconies and tortured wardrobes up staircases. Fortunately our last move was 800 kilometres, so we had to get the real thing. Two big strapping chaps and a pantechnicon.

They gave me sturdy boxes, butcher's paper and masking tape. I filled boxes and left them where they stood and wrote 'bathroom' or 'bedroom' on top. Next I stuck labels on furniture saying 'Groff Lounge' and 'Groff Kitchen', so they knew where to put things at the other end. I gave money to the neighbour's housekeeper to clean up after us, then I got on the plane. Truly heaven.

Troubleshooting

Like camellias, men do not move well. I have found insecurity and fear to be in direct proportion to the size of the person. It's Maggie's Law.

Women, on the other hand, can't wait to arrange furniture in the new house.

THINGS YOU SHOULD KNOW

- Young children think you are actually going to move the house. They worry contents will be forgotten.
- Never, never, ever assume that old bit of wood on the floor at the back of the shed is just an old bit of wood on the floor at the back of the shed. His Nibs will have been saving it since 1974. Pack it.
- It's best to move on a weekday, when children are at school and men at work. (Gee, that'd be a good name for a band.)
- Don't start renovating the minute you move in. You need to live there for at least six months to see what works and what doesn't.
- Teenagers will not speak to you for weeks. Months! It's marvellous . . .

CHAPTER SEVENTEEN

HOW TO HOLD A STATE FUNERAL FOR A GOLDFISH

In mid-1998 I fired off the following letter to the *Sydney Morning Herald*. I use the term 'fired off' because I'm a copious letter writer. This is what happens when you fail the Girl Guides Letter Writing Badge. I was surprised my offering to the *Herald* was published whole as I felt the final paragraph begging for a publisher was cheeky in the extreme. When you've spent ten years sending manuscripts and synopses to publishing houses, and wall-papered a kitchen with rejection letters, you get desperate and try anything.

The letter's publication caused a whirlwind of response. I received calls from all over Australia. Fathers, mothers, doctors, business women and publishers called in congratulatory support.

Alan Jones, the radio announcer, interviewed me on Sydney Radio 2UE after reading the letter on air. Once again my phone ran hot, and yet again after Mr Jones replayed the interview on Brisbane radio a few weeks later.

THE LETTER
Motherhood Is More Than Just Housework

When are we going to stop the insidious devaluation of motherhood by career women who, through lack of experience, confuse the profession of motherhood with the menial task of housework? 'Stay-at-home-mum', 'housewife' and inappropriate advertising conjure images of brain-dead wastrels who bide time reading magazines while a chemical cleans their ovens.

What tommyrot! Housework has nothing to do with motherhood. Housework is care of a house. It requires little skill and benefits the family indirectly.

Motherhood is care of a family. Cooking and grocery shopping are things you do for people. They require skill and planning. Family members benefit directly.

I hope this shocking enlightenment sends a clear message to career women. Don't disparage what you don't understand.

I gave up my career to be a mother. Its instruction has no equal. I am now a caterer, administrator, accountant, mediator, nurse, painter and decorator, budget controller, vet assistant, early-childhood educator, educational assistant, landscape gardener, taxi driver, tailor, renovator, bike engineer, dance instructor, sports coach and an expert on organisation and time and motion skills. I can make dinosaurs from cardboard, do projects on the activated sludge process and make a white sauce with a baby on my hip. I can do these things three at a time. Sometimes without sleep.

What career could teach this, and give such rewards as I reap at tuck-in time? Motherhood is, indeed, the necessity of all inventions.

Oh! I almost forgot. Over ten years I have written a massive tome on motherhood, full of instructions, tips, pitfalls and 'How To's'. Is there a publisher interested in making a packet? Give me a call. Sorry, I don't have time to send out query letters, I'm holding a state funeral for a goldfish at 4 o'clock.

As I read this letter I can only sit back and wonder at its consequences. One phone call in particular touched me deeply. She didn't leave her name. And only said a few words.

'Thank you,' she sobbed. 'Oh, thank you.' Then she put down the phone. I sat on the floor and howled. It was a most humbling experience. And my finest reward.

Back to goldfish. Surprisingly I received several calls regarding their funerals. It seems not many people know the protocol. I can't imagine why.

I used to have a boyfriend, Michael, who kept carrot peelings in his pocket. His party trick was to dangle a peeling in a goldfish bowl, wiggle it around, then pluck it out and eat it. As a method for inciting riot and revulsion it has no equal. This has nothing to do with goldfish funerals. I just thought you ought to know. In case Michael emigrates.

Important Information
Goldfish know when to die. The first day of school, Christmas morning, birthdays, the first broken bone. They pick their time. Some even suicide by launching themselves from bowls onto the floor.

Gauging a child's reaction to a goldfish death is as hard to pick as a broken nose, although proximity to first day of school, Christmas morning, etc., is a good benchmark to assume catastrophic grief will ensue. When Charles, Prince of Whales, turned up his royal fins on Easter Sunday he was greeted with a few words of annoyance and promptly flushed down the U-bend with the eulogy, 'Off to Bondi'. Two months later Finneus Fish got black arm bands, a day off school and a headstone.

Damage Control
It is unusual to form a deep and meaningful relationship with a goldfish, so it's advisable to abandon high ideals of teaching children about death. Save this for important bereavements.

Assess the situation. Do you have time for grief counselling? Does the child need a new train? Do you want another fish?

Choices

1. Pretend fish is sick. Put it in a jar and say, 'I'll take it to the vet while you're at school.' Then take the body to the pet shop and purchase an identical fish. Buy weed for camouflage.
2. Explain the fish is dead. Follow immediately with: 'We will go together and buy a new one after school' or 'We will go to the toy shop now and buy a new Barbie'. The child will ask, 'Can we have a dog?' You say, 'No.'

Your Reaction

If your child is not upset you will be worried he suffers from a rare genetic uncaring disorder that will end before a judge. If your child is distressed, you will be distressed by his distress, not the death of the fish. It is therefore an immediate reaction to say, 'For heaven's sake, James, it's only a fish. Pull yourself together.' Don't do this. Let them cry oceans. Offer cuddles, biscuits and coo, 'I know, ooh I know,' just like Sybil Fawlty.

Murder

Okay. So the cat has done a spot of unlicensed fishing. There is no way to hide this event because children demand to see the body. Tell the truth and both you and the cat must enter damage control.

Disposal

1. The U-bend.
2. A state funeral.

The State Funeral

The body is washed and dried with paper towels.

It is gently laid on a bed of tissues in a small empty Whitmans chocolate box. Curtains are closed.

The death is announced via telephone to closest friends. A suitable burial spot is chosen and a hole one foot deep is dug. Music is played full volume on stereo. Albinoni's Concerto in D Minor for Oboe and Strings Opus 9 is suitably stirring. The funeral procession leaves by the front door, the leader carrying the coffin. The procession walks twice round the house quickly, as at least two members of the cortege need to use the bathroom. The coffin is lowered into the grave. Everyone throws on a bit of dirt.

'You threw a stone.'

'No, I didn't.'

'Yes you did.'

'Mum ...'

'We are gathered here today to farewell dear Jaws. He was a good fish. Goodbye, Jaws.'

'Goodbye.'

'Bye bye, Jawsie.'

The earth is piled in and flattened down. A cross made from paddle pop sticks is erected. 'Jaws' is printed on the crossbar. Flowers are picked and placed on the grave.

And, for goodness sake, don't cook fish for dinner.

Le Fin

CHAPTER EIGHTEEN

BAD BEHAVIOUR

Last week, at the supermarket checkout, I stood in a trance musing on the pros and cons of changing dentists now that old man Warboys has developed Parkinson's. In front of me a young mother clutched her new baby while jockeying into position a trolley of food to sate Ethiopia. Her two-year-old son was 'helping'. Suddenly he applied the bellows, pulled sweets off shelves, kicked the trolley and revved to crescendo. The usual.

A ripping chap in the next queue made disapproving comments, supported by finger-pointing from fellow queue mates. Model citizens to a man.

'I'd have had a good belting if I'd behaved like that,' said one.

'Perhaps that's why you're so miserable,' I politely retorted.

'Who the fuck are you?' he said.

I was about to say I was the woman who'd recently purchased a new car that wouldn't fit in our garage, when a stern female voice behind me said, 'How dare you swear in front of a child.'

Its owner, a blustery matron, pushed past me and proceeded to help the mother unload her trolley. Suitably humbled, I joined in. The matron hadn't finished. She fixed her eyes on the check-out girl. 'How dare you put sweets where you know children can see them. It's despicable!'

The check-out girl burst into tears. Probably too much high-fibre sex. The two-year-old had long since stopped screaming and was staring at us open-mouthed.

The manager arrived. Mr Smiles. Matron was on a roll. 'Take that stupid grin off your face,' she shouted. 'How dare you place temptation at checkouts, and why isn't one of your staff helping this young mother?'

Applause erupted from queues 1 through 19. It was better than 'Melrose Place'.

'Dear me,' said matron, lowering her voice. 'This supermarket has behaved very badly.'

I tell you true.

Tweed Heads is a happening place.

Things to Remember

- All children behave badly when they are hungry and/or tired. Reprimands inflame the situation.
- Your response to bad behaviour is directly related to location, other human presence, your tiredness, your state of mind and what is happening the rest of the day. It has nothing to do with the magnitude of the miscreant's wrongdoings.
- Children are naughty on windy days. Ask any school teacher.

Charlotte Warrior Bridesmaid

It's half an hour to cousin Jane's wedding and Charlotte the bridesmaid has refused to put her dress on and has thrown her posy at the page boy, hitting him in the eye. Do you really think smacking Charlotte and saying she can't go to the wedding will help? Well, it won't. Never lose sight of the desired result. And use fair means or foul to do so.

1. Cuddle the page boy and apologise on Charlotte's behalf.
2. Tell him he can take two photos with your camera.
3. Turn directly to Charlotte, cuddle her and say she can take two photos as well. (Don't cuddle too tight!)

4. Now coax, bribe and pour Charlotte into the dress. Whatever it takes. A BMW on her sixteenth birthday. Anything. As long as you win. Remember: Rewards have more power than threats.

Damage Control

Don't waste time teaching a lesson to a tired hungry child. Ignore badness. Feed and put them to bed. For damage control of misdemeanours at other times, I use my BASTARD technique. It's simple. Occasionally it works.

*B*e safe. Remove child from harm's way.
*A*nger. Control yours.
*S*eparate child from others.
*T*ell child you're upset and why.
*A*ppropriate punishment.
*R*epair. Make them apologise.
*D*rink. A big brandy, thank you.

Summary
- Remember, you are the grown-up. Copy the sign and paste it on the kitchen wall, especially if you have toddlers.
- Never lose sight of the desired result.

Copy This

I
AM
THE
GROWN-UP!

REAL BAD DUDES

These children are always physically attractive. It's nature's way of protecting them. They are disrespectful to adults, flush your things down the toilet, smear food on furniture, steal, kick you in public, break and cut other children's toys, ignore you all the time and hit and bite their playmates. They are aggressive, non-compliant and uncontrollable. They are disliked by teachers, parents and other children.

Sending the child to school early will not solve the problem. All this does is disrupt the whole class. It is not a teacher's problem. It's a case for Mulder and Scully. And other professionals.

WHEN OTHER CHILDREN ARE NAUGHTY IN YOUR HOME
Rules
1. You are in charge.
2. You are the grown-up.
3. Never smack someone else's child.

I have been tempted, over the years, to keelhaul several little ingrates who have graced our Axminster. At times I wish I knew acupuncture. Tiredness and hunger are never to blame. No. They are just plain bad.

Rotten to the core. My child would never do that in someone else's home. Ha bloody ha.

You must be seen by other children present to be dealing with the situation. Implement BASTARD technique immediately. The appropriate punishment is that you will tell their parents what they have done. Nothing more.

Of course you don't. Because mothers never do! We're so pathetic . . .

BAD HABITS

Adults have peculiar affectations known as habits, and children are no different. They are irritating to others and this is the greatest damage they do.

Some mannerisms occupy only a passing few weeks or days in a child's life, particularly ones that start in direct imitation of a classmate. These take the form of hair twirling, unattractive facial expressions, scoffing, unusual limb movements, sniffing, blinking, sighing loudly, head tossing, etc. etc.

They drive you up the wall. Ignore them and they go away. Respond in anger and they continue. The effort is all yours. Yet another thing they don't tell you in antenatal classes.

NAIL-BITING

I was a nail-biter. My mother tried everything. Gloves, disgusting medicinal applications, shame, gelatine supplements, and a host of wartime remedies. Nothing worked.

Next stop Dr Taylor. He informed my mother I had a dietary deficiency. Big mistake, Dr Taylor. Had I not needed to use the bathroom your life would have ended right there in your black leather swivel chair.

Undaunted by the Godlike power of the medical profession my mother implemented one of her innovative procedures. She marched me into Woolworths and purchased a three-foot plastic statue of the Venus de Milo.

'Look,' she said, pointing at poor armless Venus, cold and vulnerable on her plinth. 'Look, Maggie. That's what happens if you bite your nails.'

I never nibbled again. I was only five. An impressionable age ...

Prevention and Cure

Nail-biting is common. It is not a sign of bad diet. You can do a lot to stop this habit starting by keeping nails short and tidy. Often it begins by the child nibbling at a sharp bit and, hey presto, a habit develops.

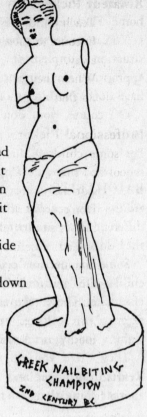

GREEK NAILBITING CHAMPION 2ND CENTURY BC

- Give jelly once a week to provide gelatine. This strengthens nails.
- Cut nails once a week and file down tempting 'levers'.
- If nails are already nibbled, check daily and clip off sharp bits.
- Purchase an offensive-tasting solution from the pharmacy. Yes, there are products specially formulated for nail-biters.

You can spend time philosophising on anxiety and the beauty of long nails, but these efforts will be wasted because once you have stopped the nail-biting it will be replaced by another bad habit. Probably this one ...

NOSE-PICKING

Q. What do you find up an empty nose?
A. Fingerprints.

Say what you will, it is immensely satisfying to remove that dried bit of mucus that is itching oh so terribly much. Men do it at traffic lights. Women do it in bathrooms. Children do it anywhere.

Amateur Pickers
- Teach child it is revolting and must be done in private.
- Encourage them to wipe the trophy on a tissue and throw it away.
- When they pick, say, 'That looks awful', rather than 'Don't do that'.

Professional Pickers
For some children this habit gets out of hand. They are teased at school and many develop scabs around the nostrils. Most fetching.
- Cut nails short to avoid nasal damage.
- Don't scold. Gently suggest it's very unpleasant. Retch a bit—that sort of thing.
- Spread Vaseline around nostrils to soften scabs—sharp dry bits are temptation for pickers.
- Give rewards for long periods of non-picking—a favourite sweet rather than a stupid star on a stupid chart, thank you very much. This will teach the child not to pick in front of you. Slowly these short periods of abstinence will lengthen. Very slowly.

Traffic Light Pickers
Listen fellas. What is it with you guys and the colour red? Show a red rag to a bull and nostrils flare. Show a red light to a man and a finger goes up the nose. Stop it.

We gals in the next cars *do not like it*. Much to my family's embarrassment, I usually wind down the window and call out, 'Wave when you get to the bridge.' One wonders what happens if they get a green light run from Sydney to Melbourne. Do they arrive breathing frantically from their mouths with noses jam-packed with boogers?

THUMB-SUCKERS
Here's the rub. A lot of thinking went into planning the human face. I mean, imagine having the foresight to put nostrils right above the mouth so there is a comfortable resting spot for the finger while sucking your thumb.

Thumb nurturing is both a comfort and a habit. Some babies suck thumbs in their mother's womb. It is not a sign of emotional disturbance, but if continued for years it may deform teeth or damage the thumbnail.

Facts
Most children grow out of thumb-sucking by themselves. The major problem is you don't like looking at it. Don't panic. Look around. How many adults do you see sucking their thumbs? Exactly.

Damage Control for Worrier Mothers
I shall treat this with the lack of gravity it demands.

- Apply nasty substance to offending digit—the treatment used to prevent nail-biting works well. It will also make your cooking seem more attractive—a definite bonus.
- Boxing gloves. Make a game of it. Ha ha and all that. Put gloves on at peak sucking times—bedtime, watching TV and car rides.

GENITAL-CLUTCHING
Twenty-five years ago, nursing on a paediatric ward in London, I had a run-in with the authorities. I'd been sitting by a little boy's bed reading a story. He kept on fiddling with his genitals.

'Winston,' I said (they have names like that in London), 'will you leave that alone?'

Unfortunately for me a young female paediatrician was passing. 'Nurse,' she said sharply, 'Winston is performing a perfectly natural function. Do you want him to be ashamed of his penis?'

I went beetroot. I was nineteen.

From somewhere I heard a voice say, 'It's very rude of Winston to play with himself while I'm sitting next to him reading a book. If Winston doesn't learn when and where to do these things he will end up in the slammer.'

I was marched off to Miss Caroline Moos, the Director of Nursing. Miss Moos agreed with me, but I was made to apologise to the doctor and Winston. That's how it was in the good old days. One was humiliated at all costs. I secretly prayed the bluebird of happiness would crap all over the paediatrician's wedding cake and I promised Winston I'd visit him in Brixton Prison.

Things seem to have got worse. Three-year-old girls know where their vagina is, but they haven't got a clue where their heart and lungs are. It's absurd.

Shoot-Troubling

- First ascertain the child does not have a urinary infection, thrush, rash irritation from soap powders or has not spent too long in wet sandy swimmers.
- Explain you understand it is pleasurable for them to touch themselves but it is not good manners to do this in public. Or in hospital! And tell them I said so.

SWEARING

There are four places to go if you want to hear top-class swearing.

1. A building site.
2. A golf course.
3. A primary school playground.
4. My sewing room.

There is nothing quite so soothing as a few Anglo-Saxon expletives when you have sewn a right sleeve into a left armhole. It lowers the blood pressure. I can swear in four languages. And ask directions to the railway station.

My first attempts were notably feeble. My mother opened the bedroom curtains to a dull and windy day. 'What a bastard morning,' I said, thrilled at my new command of the English language. It was downhill from then on.

Occasionally I have noticed children swear accidentally, not understanding the finer points of sentence construction. Driving through Cooma a few years ago we passed a takeaway chicken shop.

My daughter announced from the back seat, 'Let's stop for fucky-eyed kitty.' We stopped all right, but only because the driver had temporarily lost mastership of his vehicle.

Children know instinctively swearing is antisocial. Babies mimic mother's language. Their first words are mama, dada, ball. Not 'Oh, shit'. Why? Because they know it's wrong.

Joking aside, children need to learn swearing is ugly and offensive to peers, you, other parents and teachers. Nip in the bud before it becomes a habit.

WORSE THAN SWEARING

Occasionally my daughter will hear me swear. What she will never hear uttered by me are unpleasant much-used derogatory terms for foreign nationals or people of other sexual persuasions. These words hurt people. They do not simply offend a sensibility, as swearing does. They hurt.

STEALING

There are no funnies in this section. There is absolutely nothing humorous about stealing. Fortunately, I have no personal experience to call upon, so I discussed the matter with a psychiatrist and a member of the police force.

'Is stealing bad?' I said.

'Yes,' they said.

No doubt a two-year government-funded research program at Macquarie University has come up with the same answer.

- Don't ignore any petty pilfering.
- Don't make a big thing of it. Make a huge thing of it.
- The child must be punished.
- If a child's first attempt is successful and undetected they will do it again.
- Don't ignore suspicions that small amounts of money are disappearing from your purse.
- Question unusual belongings appearing in child's room.

Action

- Confront child straightaway. Be strong and direct.
- Tell them it is wrong and you are hurt.
- Make them give everything back and apologise. This is humiliating and part of the punishment. (You are humiliated too.)
- If they have stolen from another child, phone the parent and explain you are dealing with the situation.
- Establish a suitable punishment and follow through.
- Make it clear that if it happens again the punishment will be worse.

What If?

Yes. What if your child's belongings are pinched? After a visit from a particular friend you notice parts of games missing, small ornaments astray or absent doll's clothes. Your child has noticed too.

Never let your child think stealing can go undetected or unpunished. Tell them you will sort it out. Confront the friend directly, asking if they accidentally took a small blue ball home. Name a specific item. You will know by the child's response if they are guilty.

If they deny it, telephone the parent and ask if the blue ball was 'accidentally' taken home. Make it quite clear that the ball was not a gift and your child is fretting. If the stolen items are not returned, do not allow child to play in your house again.

Philanthropists

These are gorgeous. They give everything away. Mum's shoes, Dad's watch, their sister's hairbands. Be vigilant. If your child receives a real gold ring as a gift from Natasha you will be up for a spot of repair work.

Purchase a little something for your child to make up for their loss. Because loss it will be, as you will return the gift. And your child is too young to learn such a hard lesson.

Next give the ring back to Natasha's mother and explain what happened. Your visit will be most welcome. You will be regaled with stories of other items Natasha has given away—some unfortunately never returned. Like the charm bracelet, eh Natasha.

LYING

> *O what a tangled web we weave,*
> *When first we practise to deceive!*
>
> Sir Walter Scott, 'Marmion' 1808.

> *There is nothing I can say here,*
> *Cos you're experts through and through,*
> *On the art of simple lying,*
> *Over matters old and new.*

> *So here's a little ditty,*
> *For the ears of me and you,*
> *It's a tale of my friend Rosa,*
> *And a story that is true.*
>
> Maggie Groff, 'Mummy' 1998.

My dear friend Rosa was born with more than her fair share of truth genes. She is brutally honest, a trait that invites personal vulnerability and inspires dogged trust. I love her to bits.

Many years ago I talked her into taking a day off sick from our nursing training to visit the Tutankhamen Exhibition in London. Actually it was for a pub lunch in Marlow but I feel King Tut adds more weight to the tale. Gives it an archaeological touch.

Rosa had to telephone the ward and report in sick. Being new to the creative art of misrepresentation, she had trouble finding just the right sort of disease that would require one day off. Meanwhile I telephoned my ward and said, 'I won't be in today. I'm sick.'

Rosa was still toying with viral meningitis and Menières syndrome.

'Oh, for gawd's sake,' I said. 'Pretend you're your mother and tell them Rosa's got a stomach upset.'

She liked that. Dial. Dial. Ring. Ring.

'Hello,' said Rosa. 'This is my mother speaking . . .'

CHAPTER NINETEEN

... IN SICKNESS AND IN HEALTH

Sorry, but men are really pathetic in the minor ailment department. They're terrific with the big stuff. Brave. Heroic. Stoic. But with colds and cuts and scratches—give me a break.

Nature, with calculated foresight, gave mothers the special ingredient. No one knows what it is, but a pinch of secret wonderdust bestows strength in sickness and energy to forge ahead and care for others with scant regard to personal condition. And we will never reveal the recipe. Never. And you will never know you have it. Until you do.

A VISIT TO THE DOCTOR

It's been my experience that appointment-making in this case is nothing more than a donation to the phone company. The receptionist, having recently completed a course in attitude disorders, will slot everyone in as they arrive, regardless of appointments.

Free Advice

- Doctor's surgeries and hospital casualties are never busy during televised broadcasts of football finals. Can your disease wait that long?

- Take a list of questions with you. It's easy to forget things when you're sick or tired.
- It's a well-established fact among the nursing profession that doctors are nicer the further down the body they specialise.
- Do not allow children to play in the specially provided play area of the waiting room. The toys are working germ laboratories.
- Take a small pair of scissors so you can discreetly remove the article you want from a magazine. Tearing pages draws so much attention.

HOSPITAL

My mother was on Christmas card terms with the doctors at Portsmouth General. As a child I was in and out with fractures, appendix, dog bites, typhoid, serious lacerations and concussion. I blame television. If we'd had one I wouldn't have fallen out of so many trees.

My brother liked to vary the game. He was put in hospital and a short time later would appear in pyjamas outside our front door. He hated hospitals. I think our mother must have given him the 'face your foe' lecture because he did a one-eighty on hospitals and is now medical director of the Christie in Manchester, England.

I never remember pain or illness, but the fear of loneliness and abandonment is still with me. In the bad old days parents were encouraged to leave. Not any more, thank heavens, and if at all possible you should stay. If you can't, visit as often as possible and fill absent times with other family members.

You
- Be there as often as you can, preferably all the time.
- Appear calm and confident in front of child. (Oh yeah!)
- Be honest at all times. The child has to be able to trust you.
- If child ignores or rejects you, don't get upset. This is quite common.
- Never sneak away. Always say goodbye if you have to leave

and give child something of yours to look after until you return (sunglasses, $50 notes, etc.).

- Try to fit in with ward routine. The nurse will advise ways you can help.
- Remain with child even if your presence appears to unsettle them.
- Don't promise a going home date in case this is postponed. Surprise is best.

What You Should Take In
- A few special toys. Put child's name on them.
- A familiar book.
- Family photos.
- Security blanket if they have one.
- A thermos of gin and tonic for your fair self. With ice. (Oh, didn't you know—thermos flasks keep things cold too!)

What to Tell Nursing Staff
- Child's familiar name—Sammy instead of Samuel.
- Special words your child uses for the toilet.
- Food allergies.
- Personal idiosyncrasies such as fear of the dark or needing to sleep with security blanket.

When Child Returns Home
The child's needs must now take priority over other family members. They will be unsettled for some time after a stint in hospital. Expect some of the following:
- Aggression.
- Reversion to baby behaviour (bed wetting, needing to be fed).
- Nightmares.
- Tantrums.
- Rejection.

Ignore it all and give love by the bucket-load.

IMMUNISATION

We've all passed a lot of water since my community nursing days in the Australian bush. Much has changed, especially in the field of immunisation.

I have an admission to make. About those immunisation clinics in the Pilliga Scrub. The statistics were a bit bodgy. A lot bodgy, actually.

Some patients had, well, how shall I put it, *tails*. You see, many bush folk, living as they do a squillion miles from anywhere, viewed a trip to clinic as an outing for the whole family. A nurse with a cupboard full of dressings, lotions and potions was fair game if your pet lamb happened to have a sore foot on the same day little Hamish was having his immunisation. So they came, they saw, they conquered and every last cotton ball had to be accounted for by Nurse Maggie.

Sean Cochonnery was a pig. He came to clinic after consuming an unknown quantity of sleeping pills and six months supply of oral contraceptives. We walked Sean around, as one does with overdoses, but he kept falling over. Eventually we put him in the car and drove around instead. By the time we found a vet Sean had shown the design department at Subaru exactly what he thought of their upholstery. And recovered.

I didn't mind this four-legged invasion. If it took a dressing on a living leg of lamb to encourage one human immunisation then I took the tooking. A case of All for One and Two for a Dollar—the Health Department's dollar . . .

Warning

Before a baby receives the first immunisation at two months of age, he is at risk of contracting certain highly contagious diseases from older children who have not been immunised and have caught the disease. It is wise, therefore, to keep young babies out of the fray, and avoid waiting rooms, childcare, schools and supermarkets.

Information

Collect leaflets for diverse factual details of the immunisation schedule, safety and effectiveness of products and possible side effects. If you have concerns talk to a doctor, not your neighbour.

Research

As I write, new combination vaccines that reduce the risk of side effects are being trialled throughout the world.

Vaccines are being developed based on DNA of infectious organisms which should be safer and cheaper. Over the next few years research may yield new vaccines to combat diseases such as pneumonia and chicken pox and hopefully the required number of injections will eventually be reduced. For this reason I won't list current immunisation schedules. Everything may change in a few months.

A Small Test

Guess what is arguably the greatest scientific achievement of the twentieth century? No. Not the Fisher and Paykel two-drawer dishwasher. That's second. It's the eradication of smallpox. Yes. We have removed smallpox from the face of the earth. How did we do it?

By global immunisation.

So let's have a go at the other nasty-nasties. The Big Seven. Here's the lowdown on what they can do.

1. **Poliomyelitis** caused by invasion of gastrointestinal tract by polio virus. It is common in many overseas countries. Permanent paralysis can occur.

2. **Tetanus** caused by a toxin from bacterium present in many places, particularly soil. It enters the body via a skin wound causing muscle spasms and occasional death. Booster injections should be given every ten years throughout life. (Have you had yours?)

3. **Diphtheria** caused by a bacterium that infects the mouth, nose and throat. It can suffocate by blocking air passages and cause death from paralysis or heart failure.

4. **Whooping cough** also known as pertussis. It is caused by bacterium found in mouth, nose and throat. Highly contagious, it produces repeated coughing spasms that can last for several weeks. Complications are brain damage and death.

5. **Mumps** a common childhood disease that produces fever, headache and swelling of glands. Complications are inflammation of the brain, deafness and sterility.

6. **Rubella** also known as German measles. It is caused by a virus and produces rash and fever—usually a mild disease with speedy recovery. The most important complication is maternal rubella, where infection in the first 20 weeks of pregnancy can result in foetal deformities.

7. **Measles** a highly contagious virus causing fever, sore eyes, cough and rash. Complications are permanent damage to ears, lungs and brain. Death can occur.

Remember 'Denial' is not only a river in Egypt. It's what parents do when they refuse to immunise a child they believe is too strong and healthy to catch these life-threatening diseases.

THANKS FOR THE MAMMARIES

Breastfeeding is wonderful. A triumph of natural engineering. It's a fabulous feeling, the best source of nourishment for a baby and, as my husband points out, the milk comes in such cute containers.

It's also convenient if like me you are dragged off on a sailing holiday with a six-week-old baby. (My therapist says I'm coming along well . . .) Good, too, if you're in superb health and life is a hunky-dory daydream of idyllic time with your treasure.

But it is not convenient if you are unwell or must return to work. Then it becomes a brick tied to your ankle 24 hours a day. Apart from the logistics of pumping, preparing and storing feeds it is apparent to me that mothers who continue this fiasco for several months wear very thin. The combination of work, caring for a baby and breastfeeding depletes the body's resources and these martyrs fall apart. I'm sure nature did not intend the betterment of baby to be at mother's expense.

Then there are mothers who can't breastfeed. For them it doesn't work. They are made to feel guilty. The bosom Nazis sharpen their pointy fingers, usually in a restaurant where the sight of them feeding a two-year-old boy will cause maximum affront to a pensioner at the next table.

Good grief, half the world is wondering where its next meal is coming from, so here in the Western world with healthy milk substitutes, does it matter if you can't breastfeed? You have already given the child 40 weeks of nourishment from your body, not to mention transferring antibodies and natural immunities. So, yes, you have fed your baby. Be sad about the milk bit. But guilty? Never.

ALLERGIES

All children are allergic to tidy bedrooms, dentists, spinach and soap. For a few the list includes animals, dust, grass and other innocuous items like the washing-up. There is a tendency by the robust to dismiss allergies as ravings of the weak, feeble and self-absorbed. It's important to understand if you don't treat an allergy the victim will become weak, feeble and self-absorbed. A medical catch-22.

What Is an Allergy?
The human body has a mechanism to combat invasion. It's called the immune system. When we have a cold or injury, the system produces antibodies to fight the invader. People with a hyper-sensitive immune system produce antibodies to substances that don't bother the rest of us. They have an allergy.

What Is an Antigen?
Antigen is the name for foreign proteins that cause allergy. They are present in housemites, dust, mould, animal fur, dead skin, food, drugs, grass, flowers and many other goodies including, apparently, washing-up liquid.

What Is an Allergen?
Allergen is the term used to describe the particular antigen causing allergy. The task facing parents is to discover which allergen is causing reaction. To do this you must understand an allergic reaction.

Allergic Reaction

This occurs when the allergen meets its antibodies and battle commences. First-time exposure to the allergen will produce antibodies but no allergic reaction. It is only when the child is exposed to the allergen and the antibodies are already present that allergic reaction takes place.

It is therefore important not to dismiss a reaction to a particular allergen because the child had no ill effects from prior exposure. The symptoms that result can be one or several of the following.

- Laboured breathing that sounds wheezy (asthma).
- Weals, like bites, on the skin or a rash (urticaria or eczema).
- Vomiting, cramps and diarrhoea.
- Runny nose and eyes. Sneezing (hay fever).
- Fever and enlarged glands.

If you suspect your child has an allergy, make a list of the times it occurred, what he'd eaten, where he'd been, what he'd touched and the symptoms. Take list and child to a medical practitioner.

Anaphylaxis

A very severe allergic reaction is known as anaphylaxis. It is extremely rare. The reaction is immediate, leads to collapse, difficulty in breathing, convulsions and sometimes cardiac arrest. Seek medical help immediately.

Malingerers

Once, in panic, I asked a patient to jump up and down because I had forgotten to shake his medicine. Nowadays I use this method to spot a malingerer—if the child is well enough to jump then they're good enough for the education department.

Mothers recognise real sickness instantly. There is something unmistakable about sunken eyes and the resigned expression of defeat as a child surrenders to malady. Mothers also know children can be fine one minute and very ill the next.

This creates a dilemma when we are presented with vague stories of pain and nausea complicated by prior knowledge of a spelling test.

You won't take the right road every time, and when school phones and a stern voice says 'Jessica informs me she told you she didn't feel well this morning,' it's a real slap in the face. A black mark for mother.

The reverse happens just as often. A friend of mine took her spotty Bridget to the doctor only to be shamed with, 'Surely you recognise felt tip pen, Mrs Ward?' (Sorry, Mrs Ward, but I simply had to tell the world what a complete dill you are.)

Saturday Night Fever 11.45 p.m.

Fever is the body's response to infection. It can happen suddenly and last a few hours or several days. It usually occurs on a birthday, the day before a vacation or in a car halfway up the east coast. For this reason mothers should never go anywhere without fever-reducing medication.

What to do

- Administer fever-reducing medication as per bottle instructions.
- Provide frequent fluids.
- Place child in a tepid shower or bath (never cold).
- Reduce clothing and cover with a cool sheet.
- If temperature is still high, rinse face washers in cool water, wring out, and place in child's armpits, under knees, behind neck and on forehead. Wipe child down with another cool washer and replace others as they heat up.
- If temperature does not subside consult a doctor.

You will have heard high fevers can produce fits. This is unlikely in a baby and only a small percentage of young children have a 'febrile convulsion' from elevated temperatures. If this occurs, seek medical help immediately. The trembling, teeth chattering and goosebumps that accompany fever are not a fit.

General Nursing Care of a Sick Child (Husbands Too)

Many women approach motherhood believing healthy, well fed children do not get sick. Ha! They are in for a surprise. All children get sick, and very often too. Most childhood illnesses are mild and fleeting, but their frequency is astounding. So be warned.

- Accept you won't sleep for a day or two.
- Cancel appointments—you'll be too tired to go.
- Do all the washing. Ignore other household chores.
- Prepare sick room. Remove toys and tripoverables and clear a surface beside bed.
- Place pillow in large plastic bag and cover with towel. This absorbs sweat and is easier to change quickly.
- Place plastic protector and a bath towel across the bed under child's body. They often have 'accidents' when ill.
- Place tissues and bowl on bedside table in case of vomiting.
- Provide plenty of fluids but don't leave a jug and glass à la hospital because child will knock it over.
- Place large bath towel on the floor beside bed. Children like to throw-up beside beds. Dogs too.
- Sick children are frightened children. Stay with them as much as possible or at least let them hear you.
- Keep child clean and cool. Help with a shower or bath. They will revert to babyhood and need to be washed. (Yes, husbands too.) Children often fall asleep after a bath.
- Leave light on at night, particularly in bathroom. Sickness always seems worse in the dark.
- Open windows. Sick children need fresh air.
- Change child's clothing regularly. (The washing is piling up . . .)
- Offer small 'tastings' of food. Sick people do not need huge ham sandwiches. A little cracker with a thin sliver of cheese is more appealing. One strawberry and three grapes go down easier than a vat of broth.
- Give child something to look forward to when better. No, not going back to school. Something nice.
- Very sick children don't need entertaining, but those on the mend require a few distractions. Spoken tapes such as *Alice in Wonderland* are useful. I'm afraid you are the other distractions.

- Don't give child a bell. They will ring too often and run the risk of serious facial bedsores as you try to force the bell up their nose.

MINOR ELECTIVE SURGERY IN THE HOME
Splinters
Some splinters may need to be removed by professionals, but most offending slivers can be safely extracted in the home. There is something immensely satisfying about waving a sharp needle in front of the person who's pulled the heads off your Michaelmas daisies ...

Method 1
- Put child in front of TV.
- Dip end of needle in antiseptic solution.
- Do not show needle to child. (Sorry!)
- Rub ice-cube gently over splinter to freeze skin.
- When skin is numb, extract splinter.

Method 2—effective if splinter is slightly exposed.
- Place sticky part of plaster directly over splinter.
- Leave for several hours. When child is distracted firmly peel plaster off. Hopefully splinter has adhered to plaster and comes out.

Method 3—for deep splinters.
- Spread small amount of magnesium sulphate paste (drawing paste available from pharmacy) onto soft area of plaster and stick over splinter. Renew every 12 hours until splinter is 'drawn' out.

Mademoiselle Flaction's Blister Therapy
The Swiss make the best chocolate, best watches, best cuckoo clocks and have the best method of blister therapy I've encountered. Like many remedies in La Suisse it is totally obscure. Mlle Flaction at Hôpital Nestlé taught me this one.

- Thread sterilised needle with about 25 cm of cotton.
- Carefully push needle into one side of blister and poke out other side. (This doesn't hurt).
- Pull needle through, leaving half the cotton on each side of blister.
- The cotton is left to absorb fluid from the blister.
- When this is done, clip cotton off next to skin on one side and gently pull out the other. Do not pull exposed cotton *through* the blister.
- The outside skin will now collapse against raw surface—a very crude skin graft.
- Cover with dressing and leave for several days.

My apologies to Thorntons of Liverpool, England, who do make the best chocolates in the world. I bet you haven't tried them.

CRACKS AND THWACKS

There you are, at the sink, washing a cake tin and gazing out upon children as they laugh and play on the trampoline. A perfect family. If only Roland Pickworthy could see you now. He'd know how happy you could have made him ...

THUD, CRACK, AAAAH. 'Muuuum!'

Typical. A broken wrist. On your watch, too.

- Immobilise affected limb. Arms and wrists can be placed across chest Napoleon fashion, and a jumper pulled over the top (without using sleeve) to hold arm firm against the body.
- Place ice-pack over injured area to reduce swelling. If you don't have an ice-pack use a packet of frozen peas.
- Do not give food or liquids in case child requires anaesthetic.
- Go to doctor or hospital.
- Do not rearrange husband's facial features when he asks, 'What were you doing?' Be secure in the knowledge Roland Pickworthy would have said the same thing.

Head Injury

If your child has hit their head, watch them like a hawk. Any sign of headache, swelling, double vision or vomiting and you should seek medical help immediately.

FOREIGN BODIES

Ears

You're off to the airport in two hours and Daniel has pushed a shirt button in his ear. Don't panic. It can't go into his head. The eardrum is in the way. Don't poke anything in trying to dig it out—you could damage the eardrum but, if you can see the button, try extracting with tweezers. If not, tilt child's head and fill ear with olive oil. Hopefully the button will float out. If it doesn't you will have to seek professional help.

Eyes

Children rarely poke anything in their eyes on purpose. I mean, would anyone? They are often hysterical so you'll need to calm them first. Pull down lower lid and try to remove foreign body with corner of wet tissue. Failing this, pull the upper lid gently over the lower lid by grasping the upper lashes. This allows the lower lashes to 'sweep' the inside.

Eye Bath

These deformed little egg cups are used to flush foreign bodies and chemicals from the eye. Fill eye bath to very top with cool tap water and bend child's head over so rim of bath is flush with skin around eye. Tell child to open and close eye several times.

Sometimes a child will not use the eyebath. Sometimes you don't have one. Fill sink with cool water and tell child to plunge their face into water and look for goldfish. This is the method I was taught in 1972. In nearly thirty years I haven't met one child who believes there are goldfish in the sink. For this reason I put my child under a shower or in the swimming pool.

Nose

Make child blow their nose. If offending item doesn't dislodge, take them to the doctor.

TOP TIPS

- Always buy two bottles of analgesic/fever-reducing medicine for children. Then you won't run out at 2 a.m.
- When a child is hysterical, force their clenched fists under a cold tap on full blast. This shocks them and is rather kinder than a slap in the face.
- Get to know your pharmacist. They are very knowledgeable and have a wealth of information and treatment for minor ailments. Many can prescribe small amounts of medications not available over the counter.
- Children pick up germs from:
  doctors' waiting rooms;
  supermarket trolley handles;
  childcare centres (working parents frequently send sick children to childcare).
- On hot humid tropical nights I keep several sheets in a plastic bag in the fridge. It's helpful for bothered little sleepers. Fevers too.
- Male bed wetters soak the top bedding as well as the bottom. Instead of a sheet on top, use a good quality nylon shower curtain to protect blankets. This can also be sewn to a sheet to form a protective side for a doona or continental quilt.
- Give child an ice-cube to suck before administering nasty-tasting medicine. It freezes taste-buds for just long enough.
- If you need an ice-pack in a hurry and don't have one, put ice-cubes in a plastic bag or use a packet of frozen vegetables.
- Corn chips occasionally give children a sore throat the next morning. This disappears quickly.
- Cover naked child in sun lotion before going to beach.
- A cold shower before bedtime will calm itchy skin and bites, assisting sleep.

- Write number of nearest Poison Centre near the phone. When child has swallowed something odd you will need to contact them quickly. Inform them what the child has eaten and they will tell you what to do.
- Child needs earplugs for swimming and you've lost them? Use a lump of Blu-Tack but don't push it in too far.

CHAPTER TWENTY

BOTHERSOME BADDIES AND NIGHTTIME NASTIES

I thought I'd start this chapter with something disgusting. I've just removed a dead cane toad from the garage, and that was pretty disgusting, so I'm sharing the mood around a bit while waiting for Ranger Roger to come and remove the serpent that killed the toad in the first place. I think I'll ask for a pet mongoose for Christmas this year.

Nurse Maggie is   IN

DIARRHOEA AND VOMITING (D AND V)

The most common cause of D and V is a gut infection called gastroenteritis. Vomiting may last several hours and diarrhoea for three or four days. It is the body's method of flushing out unwanted germs, and for this reason it is best to let nature take its course. (This, from the same maker who thought up kissing. I ask you.)

Dehydration is an ever present danger with D and V, especially for babies, small children, and you when you're an old folk. Medical help should be sought immediately.

Signs of Dehydration
- Urinary output reduces.
- Continual vomiting.
- Sunken eyes with dark shadows underneath.
- Dry mouth, tongue and lips. No tears.
- Skin is dry.
- Child looks withdrawn and sleepy.

Rehydration is also essential for mild cases of D and V
- If you don't have a packet of oral rehydration solution (available from pharmacists), you can safely use water and lemonade or Coca-Cola.
- Take top off bottle and allow liquid to go flat. I like to add a pinch of salt for older children. You cannot taste this in Coca-Cola—much. For babies, don't add salt, but dilute with half water.
- Give small amounts at frequent intervals.
- Do not give fruit juice to anyone with diarrhoea.
- Resume normal feeding slowly. Solids introduced too quickly can exacerbate the problem. Start with dry toast, crackers or boiled rice, not hamburger and chips.

That's enough about *action*. Let's talk about *impaction*.

A HARD DAY AT THE ORIFICE
Innuendo is not an Italian suppository. It's what doctors and mothers-in-law do when they declare constipation is caused by bad diet and waggle pointy fingers at mother. It's not always mother's fault. So read on, Macduff . . .

How the Bowel Works
Food and liquid pass through the digestive system in a sort of shunting moon walk. By the time faeces arrive at the rectum most fluid has been reabsorbed leaving enough moisture to make it soft and easy to pass, nature's way of ensuring your bottom doesn't slam

shut afterwards. Nerve endings recognise bulk in the rectum and signal for evacuation and, hey presto, it's out. Except sometimes it isn't.

What is Constipation?

Constipation is the inability to pass hardened faeces. It has nothing to do with regularity. Some people go every day like the 8.20 from Paddington, others twice a week. As long as faeces are softish, there is no problem.

Causes of Constipation

1. Children ignore nerve-ending signals to evacuate. They 'hang on' and faeces become harder and increase in volume, making evacuation painful and often impossible. They ignore signals for several reasons, the most obvious being they are busy playing.

   Other reasons include:
   - It is not convenient to go (signal often happens 4 km from nearest toilet).
   - In a hurry.
   - School toilets are dirty and offputting (very common cause).
   - Lack of privacy.
   - Don't wish to make a smell in someone else's house.
   - They have hung on so long they know it will hurt.
   - They have a small tear or 'fissure' from passing a previous monster mass.

2. A diet lacking in fibre and liquids. Nothing, but nothing, gets Mum's dander up more than someone criticising her parenting, so before you go to finger-pointers, ask yourself if maybe your cherub's body doesn't require more fibre and water than others.

Signs of Constipation
- Distended abdomen.
- Quick trips to toilet and no flushing.

- Tummy ache.
- Continual soiling in pants. The occasional skid mark can be put down to bad wiping but repeated stains indicate leakage around mass.
- Frequent small amounts of diarrhoea. This is leakage of new faeces entering rectum and passing around the obstruction.

N.B. Bad breath and irritability are not signs of constipation.

Do-Do's

1. A diet containing plenty of fluids, fruit, vegetables, wholegrain cereals and bread. Bran for breakfast is a must for the constipated. Orange juice and a bowl of prunes are nature's dynamite.
2. If your child is ignoring the call of nature, doesn't like school toilets or want to make a smell, try giving them private time *after* breakfast on the toilet. My friend Jennifer went to boarding school where the toilets were always disgusting. She used to hang on until Saturday afternoons and stagger up to the village library and use their facilities. Jennifer coined the phrase 'helluva week'. Sorry, Jenny. This story's been itching to get out for years.
3. Gentle massage of the tummy, especially after a warm bath, often does the trick.
4. Some children's bowels react violently to immersion in cold water. This is why one occasionally sees Richard the Thirds floating in swimming pools. N.B. Sensible mothers learn not to get wet themselves until they have dragged little Marcus off to the toilet. They also learn to sit in front of the public conveniences at the beach.

If the above have failed, it's time to visit a finger-pointer.

For 'one-off' situations, the pharmacist will help. Frequent constipation will require a visit to the doctor. He may prescribe a mild laxative. Sometimes the child has a small tear around the anus that has bled. Don't panic. Don't panic. These heal quickly. The doctor can give you anaesthetic ointment to relieve pain while it is healing.

Babies
You don't have to be Einstein to figure out when a baby is constipated—lack of evidence, yer honour. Regularity is not important. Look at the baby. If it's happy and well and going three times a day or once in three days, as long as the motion is abundant and soft there's no problem. Breastfed babies rarely get constipated. Those on bottles and solids occasionally do. Increase intake of water and give diluted orange or prune juice to facilitate action.

KAPOW!
Here's a little bathroom humour to enjoy with your coffee.

Twenty-odd years ago I nursed in the French part of Switzerland at the University Hospital in Lausanne. An important professor from Berne was visiting our rehabilitation unit and I was chosen for the meet and greet ceremony.

I took a crash course in German from one of the Greek doctors, a psychiatrist named George Tsaras (you don't forget these things).

Professor Soudin arrived. I shook his hand and announced, 'Haben Sie Stuhlgang gehabt?'

He smiled sweetly and replied in perfect English, 'Yes, I have. Thank you for asking.'

The entourage were laid to waste on the linoleum, helpless with laughter. Why? Well, it's what you do when a prim little miss asks a visiting professor if he's had his bowels open today. Don't worry. I killed the psychiatrist.

A QUICK GUIDE TO BOTHERSOME BADDIES
CHICKEN POX
Incubation period 13 to 17 days. A cold followed by groups of raised red spots which appear one after the other on scalp, face, trunk, limbs and inside mouth. Spots turn into clear blisters and dry up and scab.

Child is infectious until scabs have disappeared and for at least seven days from onset of illness.

The pharmacist will provide you with a soothing lotion for the spots. Don't allow child to scratch off scabs as this may lead to scarring. Don't put medication on facial spots unless you have consulted a doctor.

GERMAN MEASLES
Incubation period two to three weeks. A cold, swollen glands behind ears, headache and joint pains. This is followed by a small pinhead rash usually starting on the face, which lasts from a few hours to several days. Infectious until child has recovered and for at least four days after rash appears.

GLANDULAR FEVER
Incubation period four to six weeks. Headache, sore throat and fatigue. Skin rashes can also occur. It is also known as mono, infectious mononucleosis and the kissing disease.

MUMPS
Incubation two to three weeks. Fever, loss of appetite, headache, aches and pains and swelling or soreness in jaw and neck area. Infectious for nine days after appearance of swelling.

SCARLET FEVER
Incubation period two to four days. Sore throat, headache, fever and vomiting. A generalised bright red rash appears 24 to 72 hours later. Infectious until child has recovered or at least seven days from onset of illness.

MEASLES

Incubation period seven to 18 days. Fever, cough, runny nose and red, sore eyes. A rash appears in three to seven days with spots on forehead, neck and cheeks. Infectious for at least four days from onset of rash. Small white spots can often be seen inside the mouth. These may disappear when rash comes out.

WHOOPING COUGH

Incubation period seven to 14 days. Starts as short dry cough which becomes more severe. 'Whoop' sound is heard as child draws in breath between coughing spasms. Vomiting is common and cough may last several weeks. This is highly contagious and child is considered infectious for several weeks. It is important to see the doctor. Antibiotics may be prescribed.

CONJUNCTIVITIS

Incubation period 24 to 72 hours. Red, watery, sticky eyes that can be painful. Child should see the doctor and be kept home until discharge from eyes has stopped. Eyes can be bathed every few hours with cotton wool balls and a weak salt solution. Never use cotton ball on both sides—a fresh one for each eye, please.

IMPETIGO

Also known as school sores. Incubation period is variable, usually four to ten days. Starts as small red spots which change to blisters, enlarge and become pus-filled and encrusted. Hands, face and scalp are most commonly affected. See your doctor for treatment. Sores should be kept covered in public.

RINGWORM

Incubation ten to 14 days. Ringworm can occur on the scalp or skin. If on the scalp, it begins as a small bald scaly patch and hair will be brittle and broken. On the skin there is a scaly patch with a faint pink ring around the edge. Inflammation and crusting may also be present. See your pharmacist for suitable treatment and keep sore covered while at school. Check pets regularly for signs of ringworm.

SCABIES

Incubation period is variable from days to weeks. Severe itchiness, particularly at night, on wrists, armpits, buttocks, between fingers and toes, in the groin and around the genitals. Scratched-open skin may cause pus-filled sores. Scabies is caused by a tiny mite that burrows under the skin and occasionally little tunnels can be seen leading to an itchy spot. See the pharmacist immediately, commence treatment and notify the school. Wash bedlinen, towels, etc. as advised by pharmacist.

HEADLICE

I defy you not to scratch while reading this. Lice are insects that live on the human scalp. They vary from flesh colour to brown and are hard to see. They lay eggs (nits) which 'glue' themselves to the hair. These eggs are whitish and the size of a grain of salt. If they are close to the scalp it is a recent infestation. Every centimetre up the hair indicates a month of infestation—you can count and see what a bad mother you are.

Headlice are not a reflection of bad hygiene—in fact they seem to prefer clean, healthy hair. They are very common among children.

Signs
- Fine black powder on pillow (lice faeces).
- Lice may be seen moving quickly amongst hair.
- White specks (nits) stuck to hair near the base.
- A very itchy scalp.

Begin treatment immediately. See local pharmacist for the current effective products. Follow directions precisely. It is a good idea to treat all family members at the same time. After rinsing hair, remove eggs with a fine-tooth 'nit' comb, an instrument of torture available from most pharmacies. This is fiddly, but it's the only way to remove eggs. Repeat headlice treatment in one week to ensure eggs that may have hatched are destroyed. Wash bedlinen, combs and brushes in hot water (I use headlice shampoo for this, too).

Tips
- Don't overwash your child's hair. Lice seem to show an aversion for dirty hair, so try washing on Friday nights so hair is not ultra clean on school days.
- I use hairspray on my daughter's hair if there is an outbreak of headlice at school. This seems to offer some protection.
- Always keep long hair tied back.
- To keep solution out of eyes put swimming goggles on child (use these in the shower, too, if your little one doesn't like water in her eyes).

I can't let the subject of headlice go by without telling you about Charlotte, a proud Aboriginal matriarch who brought many children to the immunisation clinic. I often visited her and the extended brood she cared for at their home under a cotton tarpaulin beside the Namoi River.

One day Charlotte asked me to look at the children's heads because they were scratching. Sure enough I found tell-tale white eggs. 'They've got headlice,' I announced with pride.

I thought Charlotte was going to poleaxe me. I gave her the 'anyone can get them' talk but it didn't touch base.

Charlotte and I set about filling jugs and buckets from the river, massaging copious quantities of Quellada onto unhelpful heads and combing out eggs. It took several days to eliminate the little devils (the nits, not the children).

A few weeks later I saw Charlotte in town, a term we used loosely to describe the CWA hall cum doctor's surgery and the post office cum bank. Oh yes, and a phone box. Charlotte asked if I'd run her and four of the children home if I was going that way. I was, so we put two chickens and the dead goanna in the back of the station wagon and piled in.

It was a thundering hot day and I had the air-conditioning on. Nevertheless Charlotte insisted on having the windows open. After a while I noticed she and the kids were sitting cramped up against the doors with their heads out the windows like dogs taking the air.

'What the hell are you doing?' I ventured. Charlotte drew her head in just a little and frowned at me.

'We don't want to catch them 'eadlice again,' she said seriously.

'What?' I screeched.

'We got 'em off you, Sister Mate,' she explained, annoyed at having to state the obvious.

'Don't be daft, Charlotte,' I said, trying desperately to stifle giggles.

'We did, Sister,' she said, nodding her head knowingly.

'What on earth makes you think I gave them to you?'

She looked at me in exasperation. 'Sister,' she said, 'them eggs was white!'

WORMS
Important note: It is totally unnecessary to treat your child on a regular basis just in case they have worms.

What Are They?
Worms are parasites that live in the digestive system, the most common being threadworms. Eggs are passed between children if they don't wash their hands after using the toilet. The child swallows eggs and the worm hatches in the stomach. At night the worm travels to the anus, emerges and lays more eggs. The bottom is scratched, the fingers put in the mouth, and the cycle resumes.

Signs
- Itchy bottom, especially at night.
- Child is irritable.
- Threadworms may be visible in faeces.

Detection
- Put on a deerstalker hat.
- Place a pipe in your mouth.
- Shine a torch on child's bottom at night—worms are clearly visible.
- Try my mother's innovative procedure. Place sticky tape over the anus when child goes to bed. Remove in morning. Worms will be stuck to the tape. Child will scream, too.

Treatment
Worm preparations are available from a pharmacist. In some countries you may require a prescription. The cycle can also be stopped by making sure children wash hands after using the toilet. After treatment, wash nightwear and bedlinen.

COLD SORES
Cold sores are caused by Herpes Simplex virus and they usually occur around the outside of the mouth. People with cold sores should not share face cloths, towels or eating utensils as the virus can be spread to others.

There is usually a tingling burning feeling before a cold sore breaks out. A red swollen area develops with a blister which opens and weeps, then forms a scab. Cold sores are triggered by sunburn, fever, illness or being run down. (Not by a car.)

PLANTAR WARTS
Plantar warts are caused by a virus and occur on the soles of the feet. They are contagious and should be kept covered, especially in moist conditions such as swimming pools. The warts are grey, flat on the surface and may be surrounded by raised skin. They can be very painful if left untreated. Consult your doctor for an appropriate remedy.

THE BOTTOM LINE ON BABIES
CRADLE CAP

This is the unattractive brown scaly substance that appears on a baby's scalp. It does no harm—it's just an ugly blight on your little beauty. It's easy to remove with a cotton wool ball soaked in olive oil. Gently massage oil in and comb out next morning.

ORAL THRUSH

This is common in babies. It is caused by Candida Albicans fungus. White patches of 'thrush' are visible inside mouth and on tongue. Your doctor will prescribe a simple and effective anti-Candida treatment.

NAPPY RASH

Most babies get nappy rash at some point. Any infant left too long in a warm, wet nappy will develop a red sore area on their bottom. Compound this with sensitive skin, chemicals and soap residue and you have the makings of a nasty ulcerated rash which stings like hell when fresh urine is voided.

Nappies should be changed regularly, and at each change the bottom washed with fresh water and dried well. This is why I think there should be sinks in children's bedrooms. There's two years of this nonsense. If baby is prone to rash, use a skin protection cream available from the pharmacy. Avoid plastic pants as these increase heat.

Rash can be treated by leaving the nappy off—'taking the air' as it were—but this isn't always practical. The pharmacist can provide you with a healing cream, but if infection is present, such as thrush, you will need to see the doctor.

NIGHTMARES

Nightmares do no harm and they come and go through childhood like spring tides. If your child wakes screaming or in tears, go to them immediately. Hold them gently and whisper something soothing until they have fallen asleep.

NIGHT TERRORS
Night terrors are far more frightening. The child will wake and scream hysterically, and when you go to them they thrash out at you. There is a look of abject fear on their face.

A night terror relives an emotion which was real. It is not a nightmare fantasy where a tiger is about to eat you up. It is a genuine emotional replay of fear experienced from having been lost or perhaps a stay in hospital where fear was compounded with pain.

Put the light on, wake child fully and go through the bedtime ritual again, for they will be too scared to go straight back to sleep. You too.

SLEEP WALKING/SLEEP TALKING
I married a sleepwalker. I've got myself a sleeping walking sleeping talking living doll . . .

This strange behaviour tends to run in families and may I say here and now that camping at Thousand Islands on the Canadian border with the entire Groff clan is not something I'd put my hand up for again.

My husband has variations on a theme. I have woken to find him speaking ancient Hebrew to the alarm clock. The clock was balanced on his left hand in front of his face, and he was wearing the lampshade from the bedside table on his head.

Young sleepwalkers tend to take to the boards not long after falling asleep. This allows for a certain measure of safety as you are still up and can protect them. (Sometimes it's hard to tell they are asleep, as eyes are often open.)

Safety
- Secure bedroom windows.
- Sew bells on child's pyjamas.

- Alarm their bedroom door by hanging an old-fashioned bell from the ceiling so it will clang if door is opened.
- Place security gate at top of stairs.

It is not necessary to 'wake' sleepwalkers. Take them by the hand and lead them straight back to bed. And I wouldn't believe that nonsense about children growing out of it, if I were you.

MONSTERS

We had a little green monster that lived in the toy box. My daughter knew he wasn't real, but she didn't know he wasn't really there. That's how it is when you're four. And what a wonderful excuse to have mother and father dashing in and out like demented fools.

You will never win until you have got rid of the monster. We trapped our little green gremlin in a shoebox, tied it with string and then daddy put him in the car and drove to the ferry terminal. He took the ferry to Manly and cast the shoe box into the Pacific Ocean.

Now, you don't think daddy actually did all that, do you? But you're not really sure, are you? That's how it is with monsters.

CHAPTER TWENTY-ONE
HAIR AND TEETH

HAIR

I look good twice a year. That's when I have my hair cut, buy decent shampoo not on special and re-invent Maggie by styling and preening to prettydom. By the seventh day this poodle's had it, so the rest of the year I look like an army tank mechanic. Hair sneaks into a functional pony tail and a fringe is fashioned with chicken shears.

I'm a hairdresser's worst nightmare. For 25 years I had my parting on the wrong side. I don't like inane chit-chat, can't stand the smell of perm solutions and salon sinks hurt my neck.

It's why I left England. I was an embarrassment to the British Hairdressing Industry. You see, my grandmother was a model, photographed hither and yon for her magnificent hair. She advertised a product that I think was called 'Dreen'. Anyway, it was something you slapped on your head so you'd look like Nana. What a joke. Nana never put anything on her hair except co-op shampoo, a silk scarf and a silver hairbrush with real bristles. She rubbed her hair with silk to make it shine, then tucked it under a hat and went out and dug potatoes in the garden.

I inherited the digging potatoes part. And the silver hairbrush.

Experimental Hairdressing by the Under-Fives

I was on the phone when my daughter, aged three, cut her hair under the kitchen table. It was a week before Christmas so there were no photos that year. She looked like a foundling. I like to think it was this that made me cry and scream with hysteria. Something did. It couldn't be guilt that I averted my eyes for five minutes, could it?

I desperately tried to fashion something out of the remaining tufts. When I finished she looked, well, I suppose the word 'post-operative' describe it well. In panic I telephoned a hairdresser friend, Barcelona, who arrived and fixed my fixing. I blithered and blathered until Barcelona eventually said sternly, 'Maggie, it's unusual if a child doesn't cut their hair at some point.' That made me and the hedgehog feel a whole lot better. In fact by February I had recovered enough to take her out in public again.

We were in a lift at Grace Brothers when a woman smiled at me and said, 'What's your son's name?'

'Her name's Michael,' I said, 'and she's not having the operation until she's 12.'

Gentlemen Prefer Greens

Blondes don't have more fun. Leastways not in swimming pools because natural gals with matching collars and cuffs turn green as grapes when repeatedly exposed to chlorinated water. (Ha! You black-haired babes thought our life was a breeze, didn't you? Well, it isn't. It's tough. Damn tough!)

- Wash hair in Selsun shampoo. This is strong, smells unpleasant (actually it stinks) and will stain clothes and pillow cases. It may need two or three goes to remove all green tinges.
- Dissolve about six aspirin in a bowl of warm water. Rinse hair repeatedly with solution, recycling by pouring over another bowl. I lay my daughter on a table with her head hanging off the end, hold the bowl and soak hair for as long as possible, then rinse normally.
- Hairdressers occasionally stock products that remove green from hair.
- Wear a swimming cap!

HOW TO ...
Cut a Child's Fringe
- Hair must be dry.
- Comb fringe forward and stickytape down across forehead.
- Remember, hair will spring up 2 to 3 cm when tape is removed, so cut allowing for this.
- Taper fringe line down at outer edges so it doesn't look like you used stickytape as a guide!

This method strikes fear in the hearts of suburban hairdressers but, I assure you, it was the chop of choice at my London nurses' home, and it still does a roaring trade in our bathroom.

Do Hair for Ballet Exams
- All hair must be off face (no fringe).
- If hairband is to be worn, slip this over head first and leave around neck while doing hair.
- Brush copious amounts of hair conditioner or gel through hair and pull together to form a tight ponytail high up at back of head.
- Twist tail round your fingers several times, then wind round base to form bun.
- Secure firmly with hair clips.
- Cover bun with hair net and secure with more hair clips. (Child is now starting to look like an ad for the Steel Corporation.)
- Spray with copious amounts of hairspray. When dry, carefully raise hair band into position.

Okay, you can take the photos now ...

Remove Chewing Gum from Hair
- Don't try to pull out while it's gooey.
- Freeze with ice-cubes or ice-pack, and when it's rock hard break and chip it off.

Remove Tangles

- Mix a solution of half a cup of quality conditioner and half a cup of water in a spray bottle. Squirt on hair and massage in. Now brush through hair gently, spraying extra solution on stubborn tangles.
- There are several proprietary sprays that remove tangles from children's hair. They have inventive names like 'no tangles'. It may seem an unnecessary expense, but it will save much time in the morning doing little lady's hair. It's your time and you're worth the money.

Top-Knot Tips

- Ribbons easily fall out of hair. Form a bow and sew onto ponytail band.
- Regular elastic bands break hair.
- Swimming-goggles break hair when repeatedly pulled on and off.
- A small bald spot with broken hair may be ringworm.
- Blonde scalps burn easily at the beach. Beware.
- Swimming-goggles may be worn in shower by children who 'hate' water in their eyes. It's difficult, but you can wash hair around rubber strap.
- Expensive shampoo and conditioners are definitely superior to generic brands. I want to kiss the Pantene manufacturer.
- Hairdressers can tell a lot about health from hair condition. They're a much underutilised medical resource.
- Young children don't produce oil from glands until older, so hair is not greasy—just dirty.

TEETH

In a parallel universe children clean teeth twice a day with no prompting. On planet Earth we use electric cattle prods every day until high school when the desire to kiss promotes personal dental responsibility, or toothpaste is used to mask tobacco.

Unfortunately the whip hand must prevail or your child will end up with teeth like stars—they come out at night. And this is no picnic. Ask Maudie Reddy, my Mini Minor friend. I was waving her off at Haslemere Station when her teeth fell out and lodged between the pull-down window and door frame of a British Rail train.

There was a short delay on platform four, as they say, while a man with a tool box took the door apart. He remarked it was the only time he could recall an emergency cord being pulled while the train was stationary.

Facts

- There are 20 baby teeth. The first one emerges at about six months. How mothers breastfeed until their child is two years of age is beyond me. They must have nipples like boulders.
- The child will acquire 28–32 permanent teeth. These are larger and not as white as baby teeth. The first permanent teeth emerge at about six years of age. These are four molars and they come in at the back. They don't displace baby teeth.
- Baby teeth are shed at about six years of age. First ones to go are the four front incisors.
- Sugar from natural foods such as honey or oranges is just as destructive to teeth as artificial sweets. Children shouldn't suck themselves to sleep on a bottle of orange juice. Use water instead. Or teddy's arm.

Cleaning

Six months—two years.	A soft brush can be sucked by the child or gently manoeuvred around the mouth by you. There is no need to use toothpaste.
Two—six years.	Introduce a small amount of toothpaste. You will still have to clean them yourself as this needs to be done properly.
Six years—marriage.	Supervise.

Teeth should be cleaned at least twice a day. After breakfast and, more importantly, last thing at night. Flossing can be introduced as soon as practicable. Then hide floss or it will be used to tie Action Man to the coffee table.

Toothache

- Sudden sharp pain is caused by bacteria producing acid in a cavity. The pain is acid attacking the nerve. Identify painful tooth and clean out cavity with brush. If you do this the pain should subside, but will recur when child next eats, so see the dentist.
- A dull throbbing ache is probably an abscess. Head for nearest dentist or, if not possible, the doctor.

When a Tooth is Knocked Out

Rinse tooth and put it firmly back in the socket, pressing in as far as it will go. Head for nearest dentist. If you can't put the tooth in because you're a lily-livered namby-pamby, wrap it in a milk-soaked tissue and go to the dentist. A first tooth which is properly put back may last until the permanent teeth come through.

What are Fissure Seals?

The back teeth (molars) have grooves called fissures on the chewing surface. Because these fissures are difficult to clean properly with a brush, food may get stuck and decay develops. To stop this a sealant can be applied to the molar. It's simple. The fissures are cleaned and dried and the sealant applied. It will protect teeth for several years.

I can't possibly finish a section on teeth without recounting an unfortunate incident that occurred during my preliminary nurse training at St Francis Hospital, London.

I'll set the scene. Rain lashing windows. Old men wailing. Wind howling. Whistling corridors. Dead bodies in the mortuary. Vincent Price behind the admissions desk . . . Hot diggety. A real hospital.

'Johnson! Clean everyone's teeth,' ordered the Ward Sister. In three years I never heard 'Nurse' or 'Maggie' or 'please' or 'thank you' pass a Sister's lips. It was part of the deal. One hundred and fifty six weeks of total humiliation.

I surveyed 24 elderly ladies. Halitosis Hen Hussies. With baked-on rice pudding and suspicious green vegetation lurking on molars. Imagine my surprise when I discovered the first one's teeth came out. This happens when you don't have a television. You get to be 18 and don't know about dentures. It's criminal the things I wasn't told.

I assumed a nonchalant air and wandered around the ward prodding mouths. Yep. All false. I could hear my mother calling 'Make your brain work for your legs.' So I did. I donned large pink rubber gloves, a theatre gown and a sterile mask, seized a big red bucket and marched into the ward. Starting at Bed One I demanded teeth. The old girls were strangely reluctant to hand over, and several showed strong resentment when a pink rubberised glove forced its way into their mouths. At last I had a bucket of teeth, which I covered in sterile Hibitaine solution. Then I began scrubbing. And singing. And wondering why all the teeth were different ...

I was on pair 16 when a chill of terror swept over me and I realised I had no idea who the teeth belonged to. I spent much of the next two weeks mincing food in the kitchen and hiding from Matron.

CHAPTER TWENTY-TWO
CLOTHES

I wish to take this opportunity and formally apologise to members of the Country Women's Association. I have said terrible things about your crocheted coathangers. Forgive me. I know not what I say. For they are indeed a thing of value. Ugly as sin. But still a thing of value. Anyone who has picked up children's clothes from a wardrobe floor will know what I mean. For they are the only hangers, the quintessential single creative invention from which little clothes do not fall. There is, however, a golden rule. Never be seen buying them. It will damage street cred irreparably.

PERSONAL CHOICE

One fine day when the sun is high in the sky and song birds rejoice in the old oak tree, you'll pull a dress from your child's cupboard and a voice will say, 'I'm not wearing that!' What they mean is, 'I'm not going to wear that ever again and if you make me I'll ruin your entire day and probably the next 14 years as well.'

Don't react. You won't win this battle and you won't win the war. Troops at the infants' school have already fuelled the muskets. And you have no ammunition. Because there really is no reason why one shouldn't wear a fairy costume to the dentist's, just as there's no reason you shouldn't walk across a sofa in socks, or drink melted ice-cream through a straw.

It's why women, not men, are mothers. No civilised society could survive men's rules—'While you're under my roof' and all that codswallop. Lord save us pretties—we'd be made to wear sensible cardigans over backless dresses until we turned thirty and we'd never get boyfriends and never have children and the whole nature cycle would be stuffed good and proper.

I don't know how I got all that out of that. It shows how things snowball. And why *we* are in charge.

HAND-ME-DOWNS

Teenagers only wear two sorts of clothes. Extremely expensive items with a fashionable logo on the outside, or threadbare old nasties from an op shop. So why waste time? Start them young. Relish hand-me-downs and frequent recycled clothing shops—you can cut the label off designer shorts and sew it on the outside of cheaper togs.

I was lucky. My friend's daughter, Emily Nicol, was the child 'Chloe' in a long-running TV series called 'A Country Practice'. Marianne, her mother, passed wonderful clothes, real beauties, on to me. I learned a valuable lesson. Good-quality, well-made children's clothes are virtually indestructible, and they go on and on and on. Marianne's hand-me-downs have survived several children and are currently doing a little girl proud in Gosford, New South Wales. I'm sure one day a mother somewhere will be watching a TV re-run and say, 'Good heavens, Becky, that little girl on the telly is wearing your clothes . . .' I hope so.

Hand-Me-Down Rules
- Only keep the best. Pass on unwanted items to charity.
- Very special items such as 'showpiece dresses' should be returned to the original owner after use. With a small gift.
- Hand-me-downs always fit child before you think they will.

- When you give someone your hand-me-downs, ask if they want them. Some people take offence. Feeble-minded dotards and simpleton addlepates—those sort of people. Hey! Wouldn't Simpleton Addlepate be a great name for a politician? He could be friends with Casper Weinberger and Spiro Agnew.

Hot Tips
- Store used baby clothes in plastic bags inside cardboard boxes marked three months, six months, nine months, one year, etc. It makes life easier when your next child is born. Actually nothing makes life easier when your next child is born. Except servants.
- Dungarees look sweet, but are a pain for girls two to four as they have to get undressed to go to the toilet.
- When you receive a gift of new clothing from overseas, photograph child in it and send photo with thank you note. This will score numerous brownie points, particularly if sender is a relative.
- Deep drawers are no good for children's clothes. The things at the bottom are never used.
- Keep a change of child's clothes (ones they rarely wear) and an old towel in the boot of the car.
- Before a birthday party, find out what other children are wearing. Otherwise you'll have tears or last-minute tantrums.
- When a visiting child spills drink on their clothes don't offer your own child's clothes until you have asked them if it is okay. There's a chance they will embarrass you. Been there, done that.

SHOES
I vividly recall taking a ticket and queuing in a children's shoe shop in Sydney with 40 other mothers waiting to part with the federal deficit for a pair of well-fitting sensible shoes. It was chaos. All the children, except mine—naturally!—were stuffing their faces with

rubbish to keep them happy until it was their turn. And it hit me like a thunderbolt.

Half the children in the world were starving and here we were professing high ideals about a pair of feet whilst ruining their insides with chips and lollies.

I was out of there.

This is my story and I'm sticking to it. There was nothing wrong with the $10 K-Mart sneakers we took home. Or the $65 Janet Reger brassiere.

Shoe Tips
- If your child is a monster shopper, draw around foot while they are standing and take 'this' to the shop, not the child.
- Too-small socks can do as much damage as 'too-small' shoes.
- Children will trip over in shoes that are too big.
- Velcro fastenings are easiest for littlies.
- Round shoelaces do not stay tied—use flat ones.

UNISEX CLOTHES

Some parents insist on dressing boys as girls and vice-versa to eliminate sexual discrimination. You know, the girls get trucks for Christmas and the boy a doll to encourage his feminine side. Mother and father give each other sweaters hand-knitted by Inuit lesbians . . .

Go ahead. This is a great idea and will no doubt make your child a healthy well-adjusted adult and this will enable them to look after you when you're older and more nuts than you are now. •

HERE COMES THE SUN

Used alone, sunscreen is not enough to protect children from the sun. I know. Twenty years of worshipping the big yellow pie has left me with skin like a dehydrated ferret. Don't get me wrong. I'm still beautiful. To other ferrets.

- A broad-brimmed hat must be worn at all times. They should have this rule on the noticeboard at Currumbin Bird Sanctuary . . .

- Closely woven fabrics provide best protection.
- Light-coloured clothes reflect heat.
- Cotton and other natural fibres are more comfortable.
- A collar protects the neck.
- Swim tops (rash vests) that are specially made for the beach and are marked 'SPF' provide good protection.

What Is SPF?

SPF stands for Sun Protection Factor. It is a laboratory measure where an attempt is made to grade the product's ability to filter out UVB light.

SUNGLASSES

I'm a firm believer that children should wear sunglasses. Proper ones. Elastic can be attached to ends to hold them on. Hopefully a clever manufacturer will bring out a child's polarised pair, with elastic connected from edge of lens instead of side arms—for safety and comfort. Hello! Hello!

HOW TO REMOVE HEM MARKS

If you wish to let down a dress or shorts, you'll need to remove the hem mark. Personally I never bother.

- Make a solution of one cup (250 ml) hot water, half teaspoon of vinegar and quarter teaspoon of borax.
- Mix well.
- Saturate a clean cloth in solution.
- Wring out and lay cloth over hem mark on wrong side.
- Steam iron until cloth is dry.
- Brush hem when dry.

A SIMPLE SHOPPER'S TALE

'I want to speak to Examiner 45. Not to offer a bribe. No, Lordy me no. I want to rip Examiner 45's arms off, stick them in her ears and ride her like a motorbike.'

Brmmmm brmmmm brmmmm. Rev fortissimo, hang on to your hats.
Brmmmm screech brmmmm. Out on the freeway. Top speed. Heavy traffic.
Peak holiday.

'I went to the gynaecologist yesterday. I hate going to the gynaecologist.'

Brmmmm. Lean dangerously. Knees grazing tarmac.

'I'd bought new undies especially. White cotton sensible ones.'

Wind and rain lashing faces. Flies and moths. Big ones.

'I had a cervical smear. I hate having cervical smears.'

Brmmmm. Screeeeech . . .

'My legs were in stirrups. They call it lithotomy. You ever been in lithotomy, Examiner 45?'

Brmmmm. Brmmmm. Crunch.

'It's not nice is it, Examiner 45? Not nice at all.'

Behind interstate coach. Flying gravel and mud.

'Do you know what the doctor did, Examiner 45?'

Overtake caravan. Close shave. More flies. B-52s this time.

'The doctor laughed. He laughed. Ha ha hardy ha!'

Swerve dangerously. Overtake semi-trailer. Yeeeeeeoow. Wrong side of road.

'Have you ever had anyone look at your privates and laugh, Examiner 45?'

Brmmmn. Screeeech. Brmmmm. Lean and get other knee.

'It's not nice. No, siree. It's not nice at all.'

Pick up police escort. Tijuana Taxi in hot pursuit. Ten four. Full throttle.
Brmmmm . . .

'You know why he laughed, don't you, Examiner 45?'

Brmmmm. Whoops. Red light. Darn. Missed it.

'The nurse laughed, too. Ha ha ha, hee hee hee.'

Haruum, Haruum, Yeeeeeoow . . .

'She said I had a label stuck on my labia majora. She made it sound like a town on the Costa Brava.'

Dog in road. Swerve. Plague of locusts hits windshield.

'You know what that label said, don't you, Examiner 45?'

Hailstorm. Switch off headlights. Big big truck approaching.

'It said "Examiner 45". Big black print on a white background.'

Brmmmm. Brmmmm. Screeeech . . .

MOTHERS BEHAVING BADLY

'You know where it came from, don't you, Examiner 45?'
Cross to wrong side of road. Give it gas. Pitch dark now . . .
'That's right. It came from my new knickers, right where you'd
stuck it.'
Brmmmm. Screeeech. CRASH!

I do hope you're not laughing. This really happened to me. I expect
Dr Stubbins still relates the story at dinner . . .

HOW TO MAKE A FAIRY OUTFIT (THE EASY WAY)
Use your imagination with silver sprays, tinsel and sequins. You can't
use mine. It's on loan to the Tweed Heads Christmas Ballet Stage and
Scenery Development Committee.

1. Purchase a pale pink leotard. Sew tinsel or sequins around the
    neck.
2. Purchase silver, white or gold Jiffy slippers.
3. **Skirt**
    You will need about 1½ metres of pink or white netting. Fold
    netting lengthways so fold is waistline and material is
    doubled. If this is not required length for child you'll need to
    buy more fabric. Join sides together. You now have a short
    wide 'tube'. Sew a running stitch around waistline and gather
    by pulling thread gently. Leave gathering wide enough so it
    will fit over hips. Measure child's waist with 2 cm wide elastic
    waistband. Now attach elastic to outside of skirt over gathers,
    remembering to pull elastic as you sew to accommodate extra
    gathered skirt width. Hand-sew elastic edges together.
4. **Wings**
    Bend two wire coathangers into wing shapes. It's easier if you
    remove the hook above the twists with wire-cutters. Cut the
    legs off a pair of white pantyhose and cover each wing with a
    leg. Secure the wings together at the twisty bits with florist's
    wire and cotton wadding. Trim off excess pantyhose or bind
    round wadding and sew in place. Decorate by sewing tinsel

around edges or use silver spray. Wings can be attached to back of leotard with safety pins, or two elastic loops can be sewn as armholes and attached to central wadding.

5. **Wand**

Spray or paint a 45 cm piece of dowel silver. Draw around a star template onto stiff cardboard. Cut out. Spray star silver or cover with glue and sprinkle with silver glitter. Attach star to dowel with stickytape.

6. **Tiara**

These are cheap to buy, or you can purchase a headband and cover it with tinsel.

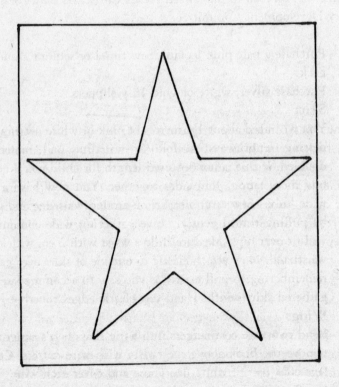

STAR TEMPLATE

MOTHERS BEHAVING BADLY

CHAPTER TWENTY-THREE

THE SISYPHEAN CHRONICLES
(WORKING MOTHERS)

Sisyphus was condemned to push a stone up hill that everlastingly rolled back again. It describes working mothers well. A jolly good word, too. Sisyphus. Kind of flows straight off the tongue.

It should also be mighty obvious, dear Sisypheans, that somewhere in our quest for equality and women's rights the point at issue went haywire and we ended up with terms the Mothers' Union finds unacceptable.

EQUALITY

The goal was wrong. Who decided the male ideal was our vision? That what men have and are is the pinnacle of exemplary existence? I made another human being in my belly. I'm different. I'm woman.

I don't think like a man. I don't smell like a man. I don't speak like a man. I don't look like a man. And, as far as I can see, man comes out of woman and spends the rest of his life trying to get back in again, and that, quite frankly, is not on my shopping list.

WHY MOTHERS WORK

I'm going to hit the verity switch. Brace yourselves. Many mothers who work do so because they have to. There! A said that needed to be saided.

Single, married or de facto, it's how bills are paid. And we'd much rather we didn't have to, thanks very much. Rarely pursuing our original career, we choose employment within school hours that is neither mentally nor physically taxing to a mistress of time and motion. Work which provides free use of a phone, a fridge for lunchtime shopping, and enables us to appear actively employed while covertly making shopping lists, writing birthday cards, photocopying knitting patterns and working out the Sunday lunch menu because Damien's new girlfriend is allergic to tomatoes.

Only mothers can do this. No other humans are capable of completing weekly paid employment targets in four hours leaving the rest of the week free for us to act as our own personal secretary. A talent we can't talk about for obvious reasons. Oh, lordy! Me an mah mouth . . .

The luxury of desire to work after childbirth is for a chosen few. Those whose career can withstand an addition to the equation, and have a nanny at home, a housekeeper, a company car and a remuneration package that provides substantial rewards. We fought for a mother's right to do this. Trouble is we won the battle for a minority.

Somewhere *au milieu* are mothers who wish to pursue their career and have to for financial reasons. They think they're lucky. Modern woman at her finest.

They're not.

Financial rewards rarely facilitate a useful support network and the career entails full-on mental functioning. What's left is a dog's breakfast of part achievement confused with mental and physical exhaustion. It's a vocal dog's breakfast, too . . .

THE VOCAL DOG'S BREAKFAST

Catchy title, eh? It is most unfortunate, but the rantings and ravings of a few well-meaning women have created a forum for discussion on the pros and cons of working mothers and childcare. Neither is open for discussion. Mothers work because they have to or want to. Working mothers need childcare. The case is closed. Okay, okay. I've been watching 'Judge Judy'.

INDOCTRINATION
Yes, the 'I' word is back. It's responsible for most of the ranting and raving from the aforementioned dog's breakfast.

From an early age women have learned that to be heard in the public domain they must qualify statements. I speak with particular authority here. I'm the world's reigning excuse maker-uperer.

Take a simple example. A man wishing to cancel a dental appointment will phone and say, 'I can't make it. Have you a vacancy tomorrow?' A woman will say, 'I'm sorry but I can't get there. The car has broken down and I've got all the shopping in the back.'

Now move the example to the workplace and you have mothers who bleat copiously of their need to fulfil personal ambitions, the necessity of mental stimulation and adult company, their morbid fear of being stuck at home and, let's not forget the real goodie, the positive benefits of companionship, independence and individuality that a child receives in childcare!

Reams of hogwash, when all they had to say was: 'I need to work. I want to work. I need childcare. And the whys and wherefores are none of your business.'

WHO'S AFRAID OF THE WORKING WOLVES?
It is an interesting exercise to read what male professionals have penned in books about working mothers. It's painfully obvious they are scared silly of offending, carrying on about time management and tiredness, occasionally hinting 'perhaps' full-time motherhood is the most beneficial situation for a child. Guys. You can stop hinting.

Most mothers know we are irreplaceable. We know children thrive on full-time mothering. We're trying to be the best mothers we can with the situation we've been given. Unfortunately the crown weighs heavy on the heads of those who must work as well.

OUR WORST ENEMY

It's us! With our own capability we have shot ourselves in the foot. Because, you see, we can do it all. And we do. It's just that the doing frays us round the edges a little. And occasionally it ruptures the seams. It's cold comfort that we execute the repairs.

I learned my lesson young. One day I was mowing in the ha ha (a sort of sunken garden below a fence—we only had one so we could say 'I'll be in the ha ha') when a branch caught in the blades and jammed the works. I cleared the debris, re-sharpened the blades and was about to lift the mower to a higher lawn, when my mother called out, 'You can't do that.' I assured her I could. 'No, you can't,' she said. 'And if I ever hear you tell your brother or father you can fix the blades I'll beat you to a jelly.'

This from the very person who taught me to fix the blades. I didn't understand then. But I do now. There is immense power in the secret knowledge of one's own capabilities.

STAND AND DELIVER

It concerns me greatly that the nurturing and careful attention lavished on a new mother has dwindled from an ocean of flowers, rest and assistance, to a trickle of same-day delivery, home to renovations and back to work in six weeks.

I fear the day is not too distant when we pull up at the drive-in maternity depot, stick our backsides through a window, pop out the progeny and drive home to await delivery of our laser-cleansed child some two hours later.

RIGHT STATION, WRONG TRAIN

It is worthy of note that most argument and research surrounding working mothers, centres on the effect it has on a child. Show me research that says a child benefits from childcare and I'll show you the childcare association that financed the research. It's totally self-serving.

But where is discussion and where is research on a mother's emotional and physical trauma when she surrenders a six-week infant to childcare as she returns to work? The same child she could not bear for anyone to touch. Or hold. Lack of statistical data on this unspoken grief is conspicuous in its absence. And the reason the shock hits a new mother with the force and devastation of a freight train.

THE PART-TIME RUSE

Returning to work part-time seems an attractive option. This isn't always so, feasibility being directly related to the type of work you do. Practical workers, such as nurses and chefs, fare well, for work is achieved within set allocated hours and nothing is taken home. Desk work and several other occupations are not so kind. The boss expects 40 hours to be jammed into 22, and before you know it you're feeding a baby propped up by cushions, juggling a phone in one hand and writing notes with the other. Meanwhile dinner is burning on the stove . . .

Part-time work can have a sting in its tail. It's the Bees Law. B^2. Be warned. Be careful.

QUALITY TIME

What a load of unmitigated tripe is spoken about Quality Time. It has nothing to do with children. Every mother in the land knows Quality Time is being home alone with a good movie on the telly and a whole box of chocolates.

THE THWARTABLES

All the children are at school and you've been offered a pleasant job that sits well with school and holidays. It should be a breeze. Ha! You haven't counted on The Thwartables.

The first month will be a nightmare as each family member and the dog invent ways to thwart your plans. Everyone will take it in turns to get sick. Something that requires round-the-clock nursing. The big end will go in the car, your spectacles will break, the dishwasher will flood and the dog will eat furniture while you're out. All children lose their bus passes.

If you make it to work you'll be phoned to collect unwell children from school or your husband will ring to say six Japanese businessmen are coming to dinner. Tonight.

OLD MOTHER TIME

The exorbitant cost of fornication in retirement is a concern for working mothers and those without forty years of super duper savings have a serious question to ask the local MP. To make it easy I'll tell you the question. Here goes.

'I would like to know what two people of the same sex do in their home that enables the government to pay them a higher aged pension than it does to Mr and Mrs Merv and Doris Greengage, retired man and woman of this parish?'

Oh! Didn't you know? Two retired men or women living together each receive the full single aged pension. So listen up, Merv and Doris. I've got bad news. That little bit of heterosexual rumpy pumpy is costing you over one hundred dollars every two weeks. I hope you're enjoying it.

Do you think the gay lobby, in their quest for the same rights as heterosexual couples, are aware of this ever so slightly discriminatory act of blatant prejudice against poor Merv and Doris for having connecting parts?

Well, bugger that for a game of raspberries.

I, as a woman, wife and mother, want the full single aged pension when I retire regardless of the sex of the person I am living with.

And I'll fight for it too. It's on my master list. Right between 'see space shuttle launch' and 'finish ballet costumes'.

THE REAL TITANS

There is a vast untapped source of knowledge and capability out there who are wasting time as receptionists and shop assistants because they do not have the necessary piece of paper to get a position worthy of their abilities. I'm talking about 'Joans'. Women who have spent twenty years rearing a family and now want to work. Female empty-nesters.

When is the business world going to wake up and realise these women can be taught anything in a short amount of time? Their loyalty, horse-sense and thoroughness are icing on the cake.

My Aunt Joan was company secretary for a corporation in London. She was also the accountant, kept the books and did catering for board meetings. When she retired, the company advertised for a replacement. Correction. Four replacements. And each position was filled by a male.

CHILDCARE

The only person who can replace a mother in caring for all a child's needs is the father. And this they do equally well, because they have the special ingredient, unconditional love. Grandparents, aunts and uncles follow in hot pursuit.

Let's get something straight. No childcare worker will love your child. The best you can hope for is a clean, safe environment with caring staff.

Childcare Centres

It's best, if you need them, to view childcare centres as a necessary part of life and set about choosing one that suits requirements. The most important factor is the centre's policy on sickness. Whether you want to know this or not, children and babies who use childcare centres get sick very often. Working parents who cannot take the day off deposit an unwell two-year-old, and before you know it there are 25 unwell children, one of whom is yours.

Family Day Care

This is a pleasant option where another mother cares for three or four children in her home. It's even better if you already know the mother.

Nannies

Hiring a full-time nanny is probably the best option. It gives constancy, stability and the child remains in their own environment. If a nanny's salary was tax deductible it would go a long way to solving childcare, sickness and financial problems that working parents face. Shall I say it again? Nah. I think they got it first time.

Nannies should be two things: extremely competent, and extremely ugly so they don't run off with your husband.

PISSPOT PETTIFOGS

I've had terrible red wine arguments with men who believe university education is a waste of time and money if a woman then remains home to care for a family. It is of note these men retain no high ideals of a woman's worth—squandered tax money is the fuel that burns the boiler.

Who better, I argue, to tackle the role of motherhood than an educated person with the essential physical criteria?

It is unnecessary, they counter, to have higher education to be a mother.

Oh really, I retort, opening another bottle. Do you not agree that future generations deserve the best care available?

Of course, they say laughingly, amused by the aggressive little feminist to port. Mothers should stay home with their children, but you don't need a university education to do that. The government is spending millions on education and millions more on social security for single mothers.

Ah, I say knowingly. Single mothers. A great drain on the privy purse.

And the costs don't end there, they spout, for no one knows single mothers better than this middle-aged tax-paying male. Their children, they add, are delinquents, the future unemployed.

Not all of them, snaps the woman on his right. There's nothing wrong with my children.

Of course not, he stammers, blushing brilliantly.

Oh no, I add. It's only the offspring of single mothers whom we pay to stay home and care for their children full-time.

Yes, he agrees. They're the troublemakers.

But I thought, I say, that you felt mothers should stay home with their children.

Well, he says, slapping his hands on the table, it's obviously more than that. It's more than staying home. It's ...

What? I ask, making eyes as big as saucers.

Well, it's, er, he says, it's the mother's level of education.

Oh really? I say in amazement. Education. Now there's a thing ...

It's practically my most favourite argument.

CHAPTER TWENTY-FOUR

BIRTHDAY PARTIES

Every year Maudie Reddy throws a birthday party for Miss Arabella
Nightingale. That's her car. The Mini Minor. Don't knock it. Maudie
makes the same cake each time, unlike yours truly who ricochets
between bright blue swimming pools with chocolate diving boards
and bottomless Barbies with edible skirts.

All my life I've been surrounded by people who are dotty about
old vehicles. To this day my father, brother and nephew make annual
pilgrimages to dribble over aged military conveyances. It came as no
surprise, when I married, to learn my husband's relatives had one of
the finest collections of antique bicycles in America. His cousins ride
penny-farthings around Old Orchard Beach, Maine. His uncle has fire
engines. Just to be different.

I started young. My mother's friend, Erica, was secretary to Lord
Montagu who, in 1952, the year of my birth, founded the Montagu
Motor Museum in Beaulieu, England. I loitered with priceless chrome,
hot-breathed the Cannstatt-Daimler and tyre-kicked a 1909 Silver
Ghost. It had a powerful effect. To this day I can take a new car, any
new car, and turn it into an antique with age spots and character in
two weeks. My husband says it's a special gift.

Miss Arabella Nightingale's birthday is 1 August. Like horses. So if your birthday is on 1 August, just think, somewhere a Mini Minor is wearing a party hat and tooting 'Happy Birthday'.

I DID IT MY WAY

Don't let anyone tell you a children's party is easy. It's on a par with trapeze work for nerverackability. You're creating memories. Respect. Admiration. Adult parties are a breeze compared to the organisation involved in feeding and entertaining eight four-year-olds.

You should expect disturbed sleep the night before and an inability to eat breakfast. I'm talking about you, not the birthday girl. When it's over you'll collapse in a heap with nervous exhaustion. We all do. We just don't tell anyone else.

About a week later you will suddenly be bathed in a warm glow of personal achievement. You did it. Here are the photos. Proof. And quite perchance you'll find yourself saying, 'No, we didn't go to the beach last Saturday. Now what were we doing? Oh, yes. I held a birthday party at home for Melanie. It was wonderful. We only invited eight children this year ...'

N.B. I only invite eight children total, including mine. If you have the same each year, you always have the right number of parfait glasses, etc.

PARTY ROOM PARTIES

Nothing wrong with paying someone else to hold the party. Children gain street cred from a McDonald's do. It's often cheaper, too. And quite the thing if you're in the middle of moving house, renovating, have a new baby or a sick relative at home. It's worth realising, though, that children don't have warm memories of these parties, the rooms are the same, colours the same, food the same etc. etc. No. Children like to see you drilled into exhaustion with party preparation. They seethe with excitement when bags of balloons appear in the shopping. Just knowing that somewhere in the kitchen is a cake and candles and prizes is right up there with Christmas Eve. As with many things, gentle anticipation is the most delicious part.

THEMES

Children love themes. It doesn't have to be elaborate. You're not doing stage sets for *Spartacus* or dressing the cast of *Les Misérables*. The theme needs to suit the age and sex of the children.

Ideas

- Teddy or doll picnic. Children bring their bears or dolls. Lay a tablecloth on the floor and set a place for each bear with a paper plate and a cup cake.
- Colour. Everyone comes in pink. Hang pink balloons, pink streamers and prepare pinkish food.
- Fairy. Girls come as fairies. Boys as elves.

- Alphabet. Choose a letter. 'P'. Everyone comes as something beginning with 'P'—policeman, punk, Pocahontas. Serve 'P' food—pizza!
- Pirates. An eyepatch, scarf around the head, cardboard dagger and 'Ahoy, me hearties!'
- Fancy dress. Come as you wish.
- Spice girls. Come as your favourite 'Spice'.
- Disney. Cheap plastic masks are available at most toy stores.
- Disco. Children arrive in disco gear. Pull curtains, move back furniture and put coloured globes in lights.
- Pool party. Suitable for ages seven and up. You'll need an extra adult to stay poolside the whole time. Children come in swimmers and bring own towel.
- Slumber party. Great fun for older children (nine up) with pizza and a scary movie. Children bring sleeping bags and pillow. They all sleep on the floor in the same room.

ENTERTAINERS

Every mother worries children will be bored at her child's party. It's in our DNA. It would have been most beneficial if I'd been told this at antenatal class instead of shown a stupid exercise to prevent back pain which involved swinging buttocks from side to side whilst on my hands and knees—the very behaviour that got me into antenatal class in the first place.

This is why we hire clowns and magicians. Insurance. It's also someone else to blame if the party's a flop, which it could be if you've hired a clown or magician, but never will be if you work on one and a half hours of attractive food, games and prizes.

Why?

Well, many children are terrified of clowns for a start. This can last until age nine. I know! And children are quickly bored by magicians. Fifteen minutes is it, but no magician will come for only quarter of an hour so you have children wandering off in all directions.

I did, however, experience a wonderful party with three fairies, successful only because of the shyness and inexperience of the teenage girls in the hired fairy costumes. They were supposed to stay and play. Instead they danced in, sprinkled fairy dust on everything, flitted around the garden and quietly disappeared. Not a word was spoken. Adults, busy with food, paid no attention to the fairies, but this meant, to children, that we could not see them. The children were enthralled. My daughter still talks about it. Me too.

N.B. Play equipment, such as see-saws and mini-trampolines, can often be borrowed or hired from local playgroups.

SCHOOL DAY BIRTHDAYS

What a bummer! You've arranged a party for Saturday but feel you must do something today, the real birthday. Of course it isn't necessary to inform a child it's their birthday. Children rarely know today's date. My friend Bambi had a Machiavellian approach to these things. Her children's birthdays always fell on weekends. I remember an elderly lady asking Bambi her youngest's age. Bambi replied straight-faced, 'She's five. She just doesn't know it yet.' You'd love Bambi, she's a dream. I wish I had a dollar for each time she said, 'That doesn't suit.' Life's a big plan. And if the occasion doesn't fit the plan, then it's made to fit the plan. Lateral thinking Edward de Bono wouldn't understand. She'd run rings around Stephen Hawkin's 'big bang' theory.

Naturally it takes an expert to deceive a child, so if you're not up to scratch then I suggest you have a few presents on the day and deliver a birthday cake to school. Nothing elaborate. Simple is best.

You will need:

> *A tray.*
> *Approximately 30 bought individual lamington cakes. (One for each child in class and one for the teacher.)*
> *Candles.*
> *Matches.*
> *Paper serviettes.*

- Arrange cakes side by side on tray in shape of child's age.
- Ask the teacher beforehand if you can bring a cake.

- Arrange a time for you to deliver—after lunch is best.
- Substitute cup cakes for lamingtons. Anything, as long as the teacher doesn't have to cut it.
- Give matches, candles and serviettes to the teacher!

INVITATIONS

I can't bear dithering, so written invitations are just going through the motions as far as I'm concerned. I also think handing out invites at school is most upsetting to children not invited. Sometimes I'm so thoughtful I can't stand myself.

Two weeks before D-Day, phone each mother on the party list and ask if their child can come. Those who are unsure must be phoned again in a couple of days. Remember, you are in charge. Don't wait for call-backs. Now you will know who is coming ten days before, and can post out invitations without having the inconvenience of awaiting RSVPs. Invitation cards can be purchased, handwritten or computer-generated. All should contain:

- Date.
- Place.
- Start and finish time, i.e. 11.30 a.m. to 1.30 p.m. sharp.
- Theme, i.e. pirates, fairies, fancy dress.
- Your child's name, age, address and phone number.

N.B. When you phone the mother you can ask if they want to stay. This is a good idea for three and four-year-old parties.

TIME

Two hours is plenty of time for a birthday party. One and a half is better—fifteen minutes for presents, half an hour for food, half an hour for games and fifteen minutes for cake. 11.30 to 1 or 12 to 1.30 covers lunch hour nicely and allows for a sleep afterwards. Waiting all day for a party can delay the first drink of the day by several hours . . .

PLACE

When you grow up in England the words 'Rain stopped play' don't only apply to cricket. Many a party was postponed due to an 'unexpected' deluge. Sometimes we called it a storm or a sea fret to deceive ourselves it was different. No matter—it always put a damper on the doings.

This has made me cautious. I'm not the sort of mother who will get to the park an hour early to reserve a picnic table near play equipment. I'd worry there would be a vintage car rally in the park the day I planned the party. Or the council had removed tables for repair and painting. Or unexpectedly high lead levels were discovered in soil surrounding the play equipment . . . I have a vivid imagination when it comes to thwartables.

So we party *chez nous*. In the garden if it's fine and in the garden if it's not. Just kidding. I always plan to eat inside. The beach is not an option I would relish for a children's party. Smacks of sunstroke, sandy food and resuscitation, to me. Just like the park smacks of goings-on in public toilets and dog do on children's shoes. No. Much better at my place.

DECORATING THE ROOM

Most parties require two areas to be decorated: the food area and the play area. There is nothing as good as balloons and streamers to set a party mood.
Apart from gin.

- Twist streamers as you hang them. Don't skimp. The more the merrier.
- Hang balloons in bunches in corner of room.
- Attach two balloons to front gate. This starts excitement rolling and lets parents know where to park.

- If you are handing balloons to small children, pop a sweet inside before you blow it up. This alleviates tears if it bursts. Of course, all other children burst their balloons . . .
- Use coloured light globes to set mood.
- Remove precious breakables such as Limoges ware and the dog.

N.B. Dogs don't actually enjoy wearing red streamer bows. They do it under sufferance knowing there'll be leftovers.

MUSIC

Yep. A party ain't a party without music. Loud and continuous. Have tapes or CDs ready, suitable for child's age. What am I saying? You know that. This isn't a book for dummies. On to the next thing, Maggie.

THE TABLE

This has to look great. You can go two ways. Purchase a packet of disposable things—plastic tablecloth, cups, plates and serviettes, or colour co-ordinate it yourself. I have used a brightly coloured Indian bedspread as a tablecloth for years. I tell you, it's not so bright any more.

- Tart up each table setting with novelty whistles, a jazzy paper hat, a fancy folded serviette and a novelty straw in the cup.
- Lay out savouries so children can see them when they arrive.
- If your table is too high, see if you can borrow low tables and chairs from a playgroup or local kindergarten.

FOOD

The look of food is important. Taste is secondary. Up until the age of five children don't want much to eat. Now where did I get this rubbish from? Scrap that. The bit about not eating much. The rest is true.

There are two important things you need to know about party food. The first is that many children are very conservative in their tastes, and the second thing is who the Sam Hell cares? I work on the rule of three.

> *Three savoury.*
> *Three sweet.*
> *One cake.*

It's an infallible rule and the secret to successful party catering. I tell myself this every year.

Hints

- For small children, present savouries first and, when they are gone, put out sweets.
- At least one of each three must be pretty bloody spectacular looking.
- Remember, this is a 'party'. Fun! Time for special foods and treats. Don't listen to healthy-food Nazis. Killjoys to the last one.
- Avoid yellow food colouring. It turns children into barbarians.
- Food should be prepared ahead of time, as much as possible.

Here are two suggested menus which work well. Recipes follow.

1. Savoury

- Sausages on sticks in cucumber crocodile (spectacular). You will need two bowls of tomato sauce, one for each side of the table.
- Mini pizzas.
- A bowl of dip surrounded by sliced carrot, celery and corn chips.

Sweet

- Melon kebabs.
- Frogs in the pond (spectacular if you're five).
- Iced baby donuts (purchase these).

2. Savoury

- Sausage rolls. Purchase and cook them early. Serve with tomato sauce.
- Nachos. (Special and spectacular and interesting.)
- A bowl of dip as above but leave out corn chips.

Sweet

- Melon kebabs. When you're on a good thing stick to it.
- Strawberry parfaits. (Spectacular plus.)
- Harrods' biscuits. (Expensive but wonderful.)

Both menus hold a good balance between foods that are easy to prepare, look great and satisfy most appetites. The more you can cheat the better—remember, it's the look that counts.

CUCUMBER CROCODILE

The finished product looks like a crocodile with little sausages on sticks protruding the entire length of its back.

You will need:

> *A long thin straight continental cucumber.*
> *Toothpicks.*
> *Capers. (Sold in jars in supermarket.)*
> *Thin sausages.*

Grill sausages and slice into two cm pieces. Put a toothpick in each one.

Make a horizontal cut in the pointy end of cucumber to resemble a mouth. You'll need to cut in about five cm.

Break toothpick into three and prop open mouth with a small piece.

Attach capers with rest of toothpick to top of head to resemble eyes.

Stick sausages along back of crocodile. Fill up every space, leaving head clear.

Lastly, prop up crocodile by using toothpicks as legs.

Children love this so much you'll be doing it year after year. It can be prepared early. Allow three to four sausage pieces per child.

MINI PIZZAS

You will need:

>*Small pocket bread.*
>
>*Tomato puree.*
>
>*Grated parmesan cheese.*

Spread puree thinly on pocket bread.

Sprinkle with parmesan.

Grill until parmesan has melted.

Cook just before party. Allow one pizza per child.

DIP

Cheat. Buy it. French onion is safest for children. Place bowl in centre of large platter or circular tray covered with party serviette. Spread sliced carrots and celery around outside, interspersed with corn chips. You can slice vegetables early and keep in plastic bag in fridge. The platter also serves as nibbles for adults who have stayed.

MELON KEBABS

You will need:

>*Wooden kebab sticks.*
>
>*Watermelon—red.*
>
>*Honeydew melon—green.*
>
>*Rockmelon—orange.*
>
>*A melon-ball scoop.*

Scoop balls of each colour, avoiding pips.

Thread balls alternately onto kebab sticks.

These can be prepared early and kept covered in fridge. Allow two kebabs per child.

FROGS IN THE POND

You will need:

>*Jelly dishes. Glass ones are best.*
>
>*Two packets of blue jelly.*
>
>*Chocolate frogs.*

Prepare one packet of blue jelly and pour into dishes to half fill the bowl. Refrigerate until set.

Place one chocolate frog on each blue jelly.

Prepare next jelly packet and allow to cool before pouring over frogs. Refrigerate until set.

Make these the day before. One per child is sufficient.

ICED BABY DONUTS

What a world it is where most of us live near donut shops. You can buy boxes of pretty iced rings. Allow one donut per child.

SAUSAGE ROLLS

Purchase best-quality frozen sausage rolls. Brush with egg yolk for extra gloss and cook before party. They do not need to be warm.

NACHOS

You will need:

> Half cup of Paul Newman's Spaghetti Sauce.
> Quarter cup of sour cream.
> Pack of corn chips.
> Two cups of grated cheddar cheese.

Combine sauce and cream.

Spoon mixture over chips.

Sprinkle cheese on top.

Bake in oven for fifteen minutes. Do this just before party. It's fun and messy to eat—you'll have to show them how to attack it.

STRAWBERRY PARFAITS

You will need:

> Eight parfait glasses. (These will get a lot of use over the years.)
> Strawberry jelly.
> Packet of individual Swiss rolls.
> Strawberry dessert packet mix.
> Milk.
> Thickened cream.
> Punnet of strawberries.
> Cocktail umbrellas. (Available in supermarkets.)

Put one or two slices of Swiss roll in bottom of each parfait glass.

Prepare strawberry jelly and pour over Swiss roll, just enough to cover. Refrigerate until set.

Prepare strawberry dessert mix by adding milk as per packet instructions. Pour or spoon over jelly. Refrigerate until set. You can prepare to this stage the day before.

Whip cream until it peaks. Spoon onto parfaits. Decorate with fresh strawberries and cocktail umbrellas.

HARRODS' BISCUITS

I call these Harrods' Biscuits because it's what I do when I want to make a fabulous thing even more fabulous—I say it's from Harrods.

You will need:

> *One packet of chocolate-flavoured biscuits.*
> *Two cups of assorted sweets (jelly beans, smarties, bananas etc.)*
> *One packet of white chocolate melts.*

Lay out biscuits on a tray. (Geez. That was hard.)

Melt chocolate melts in ovenproof bowl in oven—no one I know has the right size bowl to fit over a simmering saucepan. When melted, spread over biscuits.

Now decorate biscuits with sweets, pressing them firmly into the chocolate.

You can do this the day before. Hide sweets until you need them. Then hide the biscuits.

DRINKS

There is nothing worse than preparing delicious punch for snotty-nosed brats who won't drink it. So don't bother, then you won't be upset.

- Keep drinks simple. Two bottles of lemonade and two of Coke will do eight children. If you run out make Eskimo Specials—a glass of iced water. I grew up on this. It was iced because it came from the garden hose. Oh, how I suffered.

- Use disposable cups and write names on them before the party. This is your complete contribution towards prevention of cross-infection for the day, and will keep fussy mothers quiet.

- Novelty straws are a nice touch and can be recycled for years—I'm such a cheapskate.
- Don't give party children pure orange juice. Excited, hot, full children will get one heck of a headache. There is no documentation on this. It's just fact. It will also exacerbate diarrhoea they may get from over-eating.

GAMES
Rules
- Every guest must win at least one game. You will have to use incredible subterfuge and outrageous deceit to achieve this. The trick is to keep talking loudly so no one can interrupt and dispute the umpire's decision.
- There is only one umpire. You. Fathers are too indoctrinated with fair play to understand the finer points of uncontrollable sobbing behind the bathroom door because someone didn't win a prize at Petronella's party.
- The same game can be played many times, known to umpires as practice games, until Sarah Hardy, the completely inept dillpickle who couldn't fight her way out of a paper bag, eventually wins, at which point the turn is classified as a real game and Sarah Dillpickle claims her prize.
- All prizes must be identical to avoid conflict.

Egg and Spoon Race
At Easter buy a bag of small chocolate eggs and put them away in your party box.
You will need:
> *A bag of chocolate eggs.*
> *Eight dessert spoons.*
> *Blu-Tack.*
> *String.*

Mark out start and finish lines 20 metres apart with string. Fix eggs to spoons with Blu-Tack. This avoids tears and tanties. Line children up, shout 'Ready, Teddy, Go!' and first one over finish line is the winner. Winner gets a prize and all children eat their eggs.

Pass the Parcel
The prize is wrapped loosely in repeated coatings of old birthday and Christmas paper. Don't use newspaper as print is filthy. Don't over-secure each coating—one piece of stickytape will do. Sixteen wraps for eight children. Sit children on floor in a circle. Turn on music and children pass the parcel around circle. When you stop the music, the child holding the parcel may remove one coating. Music recommences and stops until all children have removed at least one layer and prize is eventually revealed. Naturally you get to choose the winner. Children don't realise this. Most useful if you have several Sarah Dillpickles in attendance.

Musical Cushions
Place eight cushions on floor, two rows of four back to back. Start music. Children skip around cushions in a circle. When you stop the music children have to find a cushion and sit on it. After two turns, remove a cushion. Next time you stop the music, one child will be left without a cushion. They are out. Give them a jelly baby immediately. Remove another cushion and repeat until you have a winner. Make being 'out' a happy occasion. Smile, laugh and act real happy for them before stuffing a jelly baby in their mouth. No tears at my parties, what oh!

Pin the Tail on the Donkey
When I was young we played 'Pin the Moustache on Mr Royce-Jones'. He was the vicar. Yet another of my mother's innovative procedures. These days you can purchase a 'Pin the Tail' game, complete with paper donkey, tails to cut out and a blindfold.

Put each guest's name and a spot of Blu-Tack on each tail before party and attach donkey to wall at child's level. Children queue up and are given a jelly baby to occupy them. Blindfold first child in front of the donkey. Turn them around three times and leave them facing the donkey. Place a tail in their hand and tell them to stick it on the donkey's bottom. Each child has a turn and tail closest to the correct spot is the winner. You have to play this game quickly as non-players get restless—hence the jelly babies.

Donuts on a Rope
Thread eight small ring donuts on a long piece of string. Secure string about a metre from ground between two posts. Spread donuts out and stand each child next to a donut with hands behind their backs. First child to eat their donut is the winner.

Late for School Race
This is my all-time favourite children's game, but it takes a bit of preparation. The rewards of children helpless with laughter make it worthwhile.

Mark out start and finish line on ground with string. Children stand behind start line in a row. In front of each child are four items of old clothing, spaced individually between start and finish line. Clothes are put on over party clothes, so use adult items as they are both funnier and easier. First pile is old trousers, second old shirts or T-shirts, third old sweaters and fourth a hat.

I use an alarm clock to signal go. It sets the mood. Each child must now run to the first pile and put on their trousers, race to the next and don shirts, and so on until the first one is over finish line. Mostly it's just a riotous heap of laughing children. It works best with over-sixes. Don't forget to take a class photo at the end.

Mintie Hunt
I save this for emergencies. Going into overtime. That sort of thing. Hide Minties in the garden and then let the children loose. Only ever play this at the end of a party.

PRIZES
When I see a good toy on special I buy eight to put in my party box. Prizes don't have to be elaborate or expensive. Just fun. Ideas: plastic face masks, gimmicky pens or pencils, pencil sharpeners, fancy

notepads, sparkly shoelaces, a sheet of stickers, playing cards, etc. Go to a $2 shop. As long as you get eight identical prizes these emporiums are a great party shop stop.

LOLLY BAGS
Children like to take home a small bag of sweets. Correction. Children expect to take home a small bag of sweets. No sense in rocking the boat. Just do it.

Use small freezer bags or purchase lolly bags. Put eight items in each bag, two or three of which will need to be big to pad it out. I buy two big bags of mini Mars bars and Milky Ways, a bag of marshmallows, a multipack of fruit gum rolls, a bag of Chupa-Chups and a bag of jelly babies. Into each lolly bag I put one mini Mars Bar, one mini Milky Way, one packet of fruit gums, two marshmallows, one Chupa-Chup and two jelly babies.

Secure top with gift ribbon in a fancy bow and label each bag with child's name. Put them all in a pretty basket ready for take home time. You will really enjoy giving these out.

THE CAKE
Personally I think mothers should be discharged from maternity hospital with one baby and one book on how to decorate birthday cakes. After all, we aren't going to make the cake. Like everything else to do with birthdays, it's the look that counts. Whatever book you have, you can generally cheat by purchasing unfilled sponge layers from a supermarket and cutting and forming into desired shape before doing artwork. I couldn't possibly top the professionals. Oh, okay. Perhaps just a bit.

MAGGIE GROFF'S ALASKAN SURPRISE
You will need:

> 33 cm × 23 cm × 5 cm cake pan. (Lamington size.)
> 12 oz can of evaporated milk.
> Three cups of caster sugar.

Half cup of cocoa.
Half cup of margarine.
One and a half teaspoons of vanilla essence.
24 chocolate-flavoured biscuits. (Not chocolate-coated.)
Half cup of margarine. (Yes, another one!)
Two litres of vanilla ice-cream.

Put evaporated milk, sugar, cocoa and half cup of margarine in a saucepan. Bring to boil and simmer for five minutes until thick, stirring constantly.

Add vanilla essence to hot mixture and stir.

Cool.

Crush biscuits and mix with half cup of melted margarine. Press into base of cake pan.

Cut ice-cream into two cm slices and lay over base.

Pour cooled sauce over ice-cream and sprinkle with finely chopped nuts or grated chocolate. Cover and place in freezer immediately. Serve in cake pan direct from freezer. Place number of sparklers required on top and set them alight before presenting cake. Over the years I have found that five sparklers are just as impressive as twenty hours of laborious icing.

This is very rich so each child only needs a little, which is fine as there's lots left over for you.

N.B. All birthday cakes should be kept hidden until serving.

ORDER OF EVENTS

I was once asked by a mother called Eryldene if there would be 'free play' at our party. I didn't know what she meant. Still don't. I assume it's something you have if your idea of a day out with a child is lunch at a department store. And if, like Eryldene, you keep herbs and spices in alphabetical order in the pantry.

Anyway, I put 'order of events' on invitations that year. Everyone thought it very funny. Except Eryldene. She said it was clever and sure enough it appeared on her own invitations the following year.

So here it is. For Eryldene. In case she's lost the original.

1. Children arrive. Presents are opened   —15 minutes
2. Food—savoury, then sweet   —30 minutes
3. Games   —25 minutes
4. Cake   —15 minutes
5. Lolly bags to take home   — 5 minutes

Total — 90 minutes

Bye Bye. Go away.
Come again another day . . .